...ecting

"*High-Profit Prospecting* is an incredibly clear and easy-to-digest book, which is a tough feat when delivering so much actionable and tactical value to the reader. This should be considered required reading for anyone in a prospecting role, or anyone managing those in a prospecting role."

—Max Altschuler, founder of Sales Hacker

"Fantastic book that breaks down how to be successful in sales by giving you a road map that gets you to the endgame of planning for high-profit customers. Learn how to plan, how to identify what defines high profit, and how to convert prospects to customers. Heck yeah! Great read!"

—Trish Bertuzzi, chief strategist of The Bridge Group, Inc.

"Mark Hunter is right again. If you want High-Profit sales, you start with *High-Profit Prospecting*. This is the rare book that provides both the strategies and tactics you need to build an unassailable pipeline."

—Anthony Iannarino, author of *The Only Sales Guide You'll Ever Need*

"If your income relies on new business, you need to get and use *High-Profit Prospecting*. Mark Hunter gives hundreds of proven tips, scripts, and processes to find, get through to, and sell to new customers. Get it and implement it, and you'll see your new sales and income increase dramatically."

—Art Sobczak, author of *Smart Calling: Eliminate the Fear, Failure and Rejection from Cold Calling*

"The most intimidating part of sales is not the presentation, but rather the initial contact. Mark Hunter has mastered this and lays out a process for you to do the same. Your income will increase when you read and apply this book. If all you do is implement a portion of what you learn, you will still generate more business. So stop reading the endorsements and dig in! Get this wisdom now while you can make a difference for yourself and your customers."

—Jim Cathcart, author of *Relationship Selling*

"Constantly filling up that hopper of opportunities is one of the most vital activities frontline sales professionals must master in order to be successful. However, there are no prizes for creating a pregnant pipeline, bloated with unwinnable and unprofitable potential deals. Prospecting today, utilizing all of the facilities at our disposal, is both an art and a science. We should be very thankful that Mark Hunter has written what may well become the definitive guide on the subject."

—**Jonathan Farrington, CEO of Top Sales World**

"*High-Profit Prospecting* isn't a book, but rather a tool every salesperson needs to open doors and engage prospects. This is an enjoyable read with valuable takeaway messages that salespeople can—and should—immediately put into practice. Keep a highlighter handy as you read it!"

—**Lee B. Salz, sales management strategist and author of**
Hire Right, Higher Profits

"*High-Profit Prospecting* is a gift to anyone wanting to build a healthy sales pipeline. It provides the perfect combination of strategy, tactics, and motivation to get you running in the right direction in long strides with the wind at your back."

—**Jason Jordan, partner at Vantage Point Performance and author of**
Cracking the Sales Management Code

"Even the best salespeople can't sell a thing if they have no prospects. I've seen many otherwise great salespeople leave the profession of selling for that very reason. Finally, Mark Hunter offers a guide—*a bible really*—for overcoming that obstacle to success. *High-Profit Prospecting* provides a can't-miss, step-by-step approach for filling your prospect pipeline and keeping it full. If you've ever struggled with this vital part of selling, then this book was written for you. Never hesitate to prospect again. Just follow the techniques in *High-Profit Prospecting* straight to sales success."

—**Steve Keating CME, CSE, senior manager of sales and**
leadership development, Toro

"Ask yourself, 'Would I be more successful if I had more high-quality prospects?' If your answer is yes, you need to read this book. I have been in sales and sales training for more than 25 years, and I consider this one of the most important sales books I have ever read."

—**John Spence, selected as one of Trust Across America's Top**
100 business thought leaders in America

"If you want to succeed in sales, you have to spend both time and attention on prospecting. If you fail to prospect, you'll fail to produce sales. Mark Hunter will help you boost your sales performance and profitability by teaching you how to put an efficient prospecting system in place. If you want to be a top sales leader, spend time reading *High-Profit Prospecting*!"

—Laura Stack, founder of The Productivity Pro, Inc., and author of
Doing the Right Things Right

"If you don't like prospecting, you're missing out on sales. And if you hate prospecting, it's because you've never been taught to do it in a high-trust, high-payoff, highly strategic way. Mark Hunter's book shows you how to get more and better first contacts that lead to faster and bigger signed contracts. Buy a copy for everyone on your team. YES, it's *that* good!"

—David Newman, author of *Do It! Marketing*

"The best of Mark Hunter's experience in the sales industry has been condensed into one easy-to-read book. With best practices, tips and techniques, sample scripts, and a fresh look at the use of social media, *High-Profit Prospecting* is poised to become the definitive work on sales prospecting."

—Jeff Shore, sales keynote speaker and author of,
Be Bold and Win the Sale

"The popular perception that prospecting is dead is seductive, but in the end, it leads to empty pipelines and failed sales careers. In *High-Profit Prospecting*, Mark Hunter convincingly argues that prospecting has never been more essential, even in today's social media-centric marketing world. This is quite simply one of the most valuable sales books you will ever read."

—Jeff Beals, author of *Self Marketing Power* and *Selling Saturdays*

"Mark Hunter is one of the top sales experts in the world. This book will show the novice and successful veteran alike how to prospect effectively in today's technology-driven world. Mark's ideas work, and he is the master when it comes to prospecting and selling on value. A must-read for the serious sales professional of any product or service."

—Ron Karr, author of *Lead, Sell or Get Out of the Way*

"In his excellent new book, *High-Profit Prospecting*, Mark Hunter adroitly skewers the prevalent myths that have grown up around modern selling in general and prospecting in particular. Chief among these is the quantity versus quality, 'scorched earth,' approach to prospecting embraced by too many sellers. Mark provides a compelling alternative with a smart step-by-step guide any sales team can follow to identify and engage with their highest value prospects. Another gem from The Sales Hunter!"

—Andy Paul, sales leader, author and speaker

"Once again Mark takes the complex and confusing and boils it down into an easy-to-follow formula that salespeople can (and will) implement. Learning how to successfully fill and manage a sales pipeline is the #1 skill that separates top-performers from everyone else, and it's an investment that pays dividends over your entire career. Grab your highlighter and get ready to learn from a true sales master!"

—Tim Wackel, sales trainer, keynote speaker and executive presentation coach

HIGH-PROFIT

PROSPECTING

HIGH-PROFIT

PROSPECTING

Powerful Strategies to Find the Best Leads
and Drive Breakthrough Sales Results

MARK HUNTER

HarperCollins
LEADERSHIP

An Imprint of HarperCollins

High-Profit Prospecting

© 2016 Mark Hunter

Published by HarperCollins Leadership, an imprint of HarperCollins Focus LLC.

Any internet addresses, phone numbers, or company or product information printed in this book are offered as a resource and are not intended in any way to be or to imply an endorsement by HarperCollins Leadership, nor does HarperCollins Leadership vouch for the existence, content, or services of these sites, phone numbers, companies, or products beyond the life of this book.

Bulk discounts available. For details visit:
www.harpercollinsleadership.com/bulkquotes
Email: customercare@harpercollins.com

ISBN 978-0-8144-3776-6 [TP]

Printed in the United States of America

Dedicated to my wonderful wife, Ann Marie.
Thank you for making the journey special in every way.

Contents

Foreword

There is a raging epidemic in sales that is devouring sales performance, holding companies back from reaching growth objectives, wrecking sales cultures, and undermining the promising careers of sales professionals and sales leaders alike.

Today, the number one issue facing salespeople, sales leaders, executives, and entire companies is anemic—and sometimes non-existent—pipelines. It's the top complaint I get from C-level executives about their sales teams. Even as new tools and technology emerge that make identifying and connecting with prospects easier than ever, companies are struggling to get their salespeople to consistently prospect.

Prospecting skills are basic and foundational competencies for sales success. There is a direct line that connects the failure to prospect to the failure to produce sales. This is why eighty percent of salespeople who wash out and get fired in their first year do so because they are reluctant to prospect.

Yet over the past few years, I've noticed a disturbing trend: More and more self-styled "gurus" are popping up and pontificating to the sales profession that one form or another of prospecting is dead. They pander to the salespeople who are scared of, or uncomfortable with, prospecting. Left in their wake are millions of "vegetarian" salespeople (as my friend Anthony Iannarino likes to call them) who can't or won't hunt.

Across the industry spectrum, salespeople are frustrated, failing, and earning far less than they should because they don't know how to prospect, have no guidance or structure for prospecting, and are confused by the endless stream of mixed messages. Sadly, and more often than not, instead of focusing time and attention on the root causes of their sales performance problems, they spin their wheels chasing flavor-of-the-day magic pills and "easy buttons" that frustratingly never seem to make a difference.

Sales leaders, who themselves are under intense pressure to produce results, find that driving their salespeople to build bigger prospecting pipelines—in many cases with yelling, screaming, and threatening—is like pushing a rope, because their salespeople don't know what to do. Meanwhile, sales training programs rarely offer deep-dive training on prospecting. It is as if salespeople are supposed to come to the job with the innate ability to open new doors, a comprehensive set of prospecting techniques, the know-how to engage prospects across multiple prospecting channels, and the mental toughness to sustain unrelenting rejection.

The good news is that it's relatively easy to accelerate prospecting and build massively productive sales pipelines. The key is a back-to-the-basics focus on sales prospecting techniques. This new focus begins with tuning out the pseudo experts who peddle their "one-size-fits-all-easy-buttons" and turning toward masters like Mark Hunter.

Mark has helped thousands of sales professionals reach peak sales performance and is a trusted advisor to hundreds of executives and companies across the globe. He is committed to teaching real prospecting tactics and techniques that work with real prospects in the real world. Mark's been in the trenches just like you, and he knows his stuff. In this book, he will help you understand both the *why* and *how* behind the most important activity in sales. He will give you a road map for building and executing a daily prospecting plan that will get you into the front office *and* the C-suite. Step by step, you'll gain the techniques and confidence you'll need to fill your pipeline with high-quality and highly qualified prospects. Following Mark's easy-to-understand formula, you'll soon be reaching the upper echelons of your company's sales rankings. Get your highlighter out, because this is a book you'll read, re-read, and refer back to often.

It's time to put prospecting back into sales.

—JEB BLOUNT,
CEO of Sales Gravy (www.salesgravy.com/)
and author of the best-selling books *Fanatical Prospecting*
and *People Buy You*

Introduction

Your sales pipeline is about to get fatter and healthier and your sales are going to go up. Why can I state that so confidently without knowing anything about you? Because there's a little secret that every top producer in sales knows, and it's the same secret that Jeb Blount and Mark Hunter know, too: every true A-player sales hunter who consistently, quarter after quarter and year after year, delivers the numbers takes personal responsibility for identifying and creating their own sales opportunities. Sure, they're more than happy to take a qualified lead when one is presented, but they know it falls on them to ensure that their pipelines of sales opportunities are always full. And what is this great secret that keeps pipelines full? Top producers prospect—*All. The. Time.*

My passion in sales is developing new business, and I spend my days with sales teams and salespeople observing who's succeeding and who's not. Would you believe that the most common reason salespeople fail to develop enough new business is that they either don't know how to prospect or don't want to prospect? It truly is that simple. And that's why *High-Profit Prospecting* is about to change the trajectory of your sales results, your career, and your life. After reading this book, you are going to know how to prospect effectively, and even better, you are going to want to do it!

In a powerful, clear, and actionable way, Mark provides you with exactly what you need to accomplish the promise of the book's subtitle: find the best leads and drive breakthrough sales results. In a logical, easy-to-follow progression, Mark walks you through the *whys* and *hows* of effective prospecting. With a sharp sword, he slays the myths about prospecting and silences today's idiot sales "gurus" who wrongly proclaim that prospecting is dead (chapter 2). From there, he tackles your attitude, mindset, and motivation (chapter 3)—all of which are absolutely critical, because what we believe and what drives us has an even greater effect on our results than our selling skills.

Chapters 4–8 help you plan your attack, point out the pitfalls and traps along the way, provide helpful definitions (contrasting *prospects* and *suspects*), and most importantly, make the case that time is your most precious resource. Don't blow through 6. Let Mark's message soak in. Prospecting doesn't call you. There is always something more attractive, more urgent, or easier to do. If you don't carve out blocks of time for prospecting, it won't happen. And the harsh reality is that you might have a killer sales personality, the best phone technique, and sharpest sales story, but if you don't take back control of your calendar and set appointments with yourself to prospect, it won't happen. I like to say that no one defaults to prospecting mode, and Mark drives home that point as clear as day.

The meaty midsection (chapters 9–18) provides more prospecting tips, tools, and techniques than you ever hoped for. Not only does *High-Profit Prospecting* cover everything from the initial phone call all the way through über-practical voicemail strategies—and everything in between (how to use email, referrals, social media, and more)—it does so in a value-focused manner that sets you up to enhance your price and profit, not just the number of leads. Mark is a master at helping sellers protect their profits, and the genius approaches he offers in these chapters set you up right from the first contact as someone who deserves a seat at the table, because you deliver value to customers.

The balance of the book (chapters 19–23) will stretch you and raise your game to new levels. Mark shows you how to do the tough stuff: get past (or befriend) high-level gatekeepers; navigate the maze and run the gauntlet during complex enterprise-level prospecting; and determine *how* and *when* to prospect the C-suite (and when I say *when*, I mean he literally shows you the exact times of day). The material in these closing chapters is priceless. Mark shares how he masterfully prospected into the highest levels of big organizations, and he provides the roadmap and instructions so you can, too.

Are you ready to stop living in reactive mode, as a *victim* of whatever leads happen to come your way? Would you like to learn what top sales producers do day-in and day-out to keep their pipelines full? Then grab a pen and a pad and turn the page. Your pipeline, your sales, the profit you contribute to your company, and your career are about to dramatically improve.

—MIKE WEINBERG,
author of the AMACOM best-selling books
New Sales. Simplified. and *Sales Management. Simplified.*

PART I

BASIC TRUTHS ABOUT PROSPECTING

CHAPTER 1

What Does Prospecting Mean Today?

"Will you help me find more prospects?" I've been asked this question more than any other since 1998, when I began my sales consulting company after spending fifteen-plus years in sales and sales management roles for several major companies. Regardless of the company size or if the person making the request is a vice president of sales for a Fortune 500 company or a solo salesperson, the number one issue is always prospecting. Sure, I receive questions about closing and negotiating, but as I probe deeper, I discover these are problems only because of poor prospecting.

The only thing that has changed with regard to prospecting is how we go about it. The strategies I'm going to show you in this book are a culmination of years of working with thousands of salespeople across numerous industries in both business to business (B2B) and business to consumer (B2C). Ten years ago, people were asking me when I was going to write a book on prospecting. My response was, "It's not time." I'm pleased to say the time is now, and what you have here are not *theories* or *ideas,* but proven strategies. Thousands of salespeople in numerous industries and countries are now using the strategies I present in this book.

Ask yourself, "Would I be more successful if I had more prospects?" Your answer is "yes"—that's why you're reading this book. The reason salespeople ask me about prospecting is because for the vast majority of salespeople, prospecting doesn't work the way they expect it should. The strategies they are using fail to deliver the results they want. Compounding the problem is the fact that salespeople tend to be open to trying any new idea that pops up, even if the idea doesn't have much merit. I've seen this when solo salespeople and even entire sales teams suddenly embrace a hot idea, only to have it go cool in just a few weeks, leaving the pipeline empty.

It's almost embarrassing to even be asking the question of whether you would be more successful if you had more prospects. When salespeople ask the question, my answer is always a giant "Yes!" Of course they will be more successful if they improve their prospecting strategies. Prospecting *does* work in today's business world. I believe more than ever that prospecting is essential because of what the Internet is doing to the selling process.

False Hopes/False Promises

I'm sitting near the back of a hotel ballroom full of nearly two hundred salespeople and business owners listening to "sales experts" share how they were able to build their businesses effortlessly using social media and email. These "experts" are saying nobody answers the phone, and if you want to be successful in sales, you have to live and breathe social media and the Internet. Each expert lays out a plan for the audience built around creating a massive presence using social media sites, and email. "Customers will be flocking to you," the experts contend.

Every speaker seems to repeat at least ten times an hour the phrase "cold calling is dead," and each time it's said from the stage, the audience nods in approval.

The more these "sales experts" talk, the more I see how the audience is becoming mesmerized by what they are saying and even more so by the processes they use. It just seems so easy to do. If you simply buy the programs they're selling and follow each step, you too will quickly have all the prospects you can handle. Not only will you have the prospects you need, but those prospects also will become customers who will buy from you time and time again. With each passing hour, the audience is becoming more and more fixated on the strategies they're hearing from each speaker. The reason the audience is soaking this all in is because they are tired of being rejected, having phone calls ignored, and not being able to generate good prospects.

The final session of the day is a panel discussion with all of the presenters. I'm sitting watching the presenters answer each question, and I admit they're handling each one quite well, until someone asks if what they're doing is really nothing more than cold calling using email instead of the phone. I couldn't help but laugh, because the "experts" who proclaimed cold calling as being dead were still doing it. In fact, they had taken cold calling and supercharged it with the number of email blasts they were sending out.

The biggest problem with meetings and discussions like the one above is they are far too common. Rarely does a week go by that I don't receive a phone call or an email from a salesperson struggling to make a number, and they are frustrated because they've been spending hours on a wide number of social media sites. When I ask them how many calls or contacts they've made in the last several months, the answer commonly is, "I shouldn't have to, because I'm doing so much on social media sites."

Prospecting is as relevant and necessary today as it has ever been. Allowing yourself to believe you can build a huge business without having to prospect is simply crazy. The only thing that has changed is how we prospect, and that's my intent with this book—to show you how to prospect. To understand what prospecting is, let me share with you how I define the activity of prospecting:

Prospecting is an activity performed by sales and/or marketing departments to identify and qualify potential buyers.

It's Not Rocket Science

Prospecting is not a complex process. Think about that definition, and you will see it simply means finding people who *can* and *will* buy from you. The problem is too many salespeople believe that because the Internet has changed everything with regard to how people communicate, then to be effective they need to embrace the Internet. I'm all in favor of embracing the Internet, and many of the strategies shared in the book are built around leveraging its power. Even so, you cannot rely on the Internet alone. Despite how big and powerful we may believe the Internet is, it would be foolish to believe that customers will want to buy from us without any prospecting effort on our part. Prospecting is an activity every salesperson must embrace using a well-planned strategy. Sure, there are plenty of great advertising campaigns, new product releases, and raving fans who can create a lot of customers, but rarely is that sustainable long-term, especially for salespeople and companies working in the B2B sector.

Before you pass me off as somebody who is against anything the Internet and social media can do, hear me out. I'm a firm believer in leveraging every tool possible. Throughout this book, I'll share examples of how social media sites can help you prospect more effectively. Yes, social media sites can help you, but they won't do it all for you. What you will see is the impact the Internet can have regardless of whether you have a complex selling process or a short sales cycle.

When Management Is Wrong, But Thinks It's Right

While walking through John Wayne Airport one morning on my way to catch a flight, I heard someone calling out my name. I turned to see the president of a Chicago-based services company. His company sells primarily to large corporations and typically with multi-year contracts. Our paths had crossed at past industry conferences where I had spoken. The president grabbed me, said we needed to talk, and asked when he could arrange a conference call or meeting to discuss his problem.

His problem was the same one I've heard from numerous other CEOs and VPs of sales. All the money they had been spending on marketing was simply not working as well as the board and the investment companies that owned the company expected. The company had grown dramatically, and along the way, it had developed a great reputation in its industry. The problem was the industry was now stagnant. As a result, so were sales, and the investment firms were restless. The company president knew it was only time before the board began challenging him.

He went on to say how he no longer had faith in his VP of sales. I challenged him as to why, and his comment was again something I've heard from numerous others—he said his VP of sales had for several years touted how good the sales force was and how they had nothing but superstars. Truth be told, what he had weren't superstars, but merely salespeople who did a great job of responding to high-potential leads because their industry had been so hot.

During a period of solid growth, the sales team simply walked away from prospecting. They didn't feel it was necessary, because the phone kept ringing. Making matters worse, the marketing department believed all of the success the sales team was having was due to the marketing department's great marketing efforts. When business began to soften, the task was given to marketing to simply increase spending, which would lead to the return of business. After two years of increased spending by marketing, the business didn't return, because it went instead to their competitor. You see, even when times were good their competitor remained aggressive with prospecting efforts. The competitor could have taken the easy way out and stopped prospecting when times were good. In fact, they probably could have reduced head count and saved money, but they knew prospecting works and is a critical process in both the good times and bad times.

The Evolution of Prospecting

Twenty-five years ago, when I was selling in the Minneapolis market, it never took me more than one or two calls or visits to move a person from being just a lead to being a new account. When I opened my consulting company eighteen years ago, it still didn't take more than three or four telephone calls to find a prospect and ultimately land a client. Today, most salespeople would say they have zero success finding prospects using only the telephone, and it takes any number of different means to find a lead, turn them into a viable prospect, and ultimately get them to buy.

The decline of the telephone and the emergence of email and other communication tools did not cause the evolution of prospecting. Rather, what caused it to change is a shift in knowledge. When I was prospecting twenty-five years ago, I had all the knowledge about my product—if the customer wanted to know anything, they needed me. The number of options the customer could choose from was limited to what I had to offer. Today the customer has the knowledge, and along with the knowledge comes the ability to choose from any number of options and companies. The customer now has the ability to ignore you, the salesperson, because they feel you're not needed and will only waste their time. The customer feels if and when they're ready to buy, they often can make the purchase online without ever contacting a salesperson. The evolution of prospecting is not due to the number of communication methods available, but rather to the shift in who has the knowledge.

When we begin to look at how we prospect in this light, we begin to realize why prospecting is such a big problem. Salespeople and companies typically go down one of two paths when it comes to prospecting. One path is sticking with the traditional methods of prospecting centered around the telephone, email, and maybe in-person visits. The other path is by jumping into the deep end of the social media pool and putting all of their resources into generating an online presence to attract leads. Neither of those paths is truly successful on its own—you need to travel down both. The customer has access to more knowledge, so the only way to counterbalance that is by convincing the customer to have confidence in you. The greater the level of confidence the customer has in you, the greater the probability for you to make a sale. Confidence is not something that's built after the customer has decided to buy; no, confidence is something that you must establish if the lead is going to become a prospect. A prospect who does not have confidence in you is not a prospect. I'll argue they're barely a contact!

Sales Is Not a Science, It's an Art

I've laid out each chapter in this book to challenge what you're currently doing and push you into new territory. In the early chapters, I will compel you to look at your existing process and, more importantly, to think about whom your perfect customer is. A mistake far too many salespeople make is failing to identify characteristics of their perfect customers and then work backward to determine their perfect prospects. I also don't think you can copy each strategy shared and achieve superior results. Sales involves too many variables.

If sales were a science, then it would be much easier for salespeople to be successful. All they would need to do is follow the process perfectly. But I say sales is an art, and that's why so many people struggle to be successful and is especially why so many salespeople struggle with prospecting. They have an attitude about prospecting that they will only do what is necessary to make their numbers and nothing more. An attitude like that will ensure only one thing—one day you will wake up and see no sales and no pipeline.

CHAPTER 2

The Myths and Surprising Facts about Finding New Customers

Prospecting is not the mystery many people make it out to be. One time the owner of a company asked me to meet with Dennis, who ran the field sales office in Michigan. The owner shared with me that she was concerned all the business the Michigan sales office generated was from only three customers. I sat down with Dennis in his office to discuss the situation, and though he was aware of the problem, he admitted he was absolutely baffled as to how to correct it. The company operated in a dynamic industry where there were plenty of opportunities. His sales team consisted of four inside salespeople whose sole job was to take care of existing customers and prospect for more customers. Clearly, the job was not confusing at all. All four were knowledgeable about their business and their industry.

After some conversation with the four salespeople, I discovered none of them were trying to find new customers. When I asked why, each one had an excuse. One claimed they didn't know who to call; another claimed they had never been trained; another claimed they didn't have time; and the last one told me they were just plain scared. I'll give the last one credit for being honest. The other three salespeople were simply making excuses.

The problem wasn't limited to the salespeople, because Dennis, the manager, also made excuses as to why he couldn't make prospecting calls. The office was locked into a belief that prospecting was beyond what they could do. Dennis and his team allowed their fear of prospecting and/or disinterest in prospecting to go unchecked, and as a result, they did as little prospecting as possible. You might think, "How could a sales team like this exist to begin with?" Good question. Yes, it is unusual to have an entire sales team apparently paralyzed and not doing any prospecting. Typically in most organizations, there are at least a few people who will prospect.

When salespeople or sales teams run from prospecting, they tend to embrace one or more of what I see are the six great myths of prospecting. A common, yet unrealistic, belief fueling all of the myths is that at some point, new customers will magically appear and there's no reason to actually go pursue new customers. Read the myths that follow, and see if any resonate with you and inform you as to why you have struggled with prospecting.

PROSPECTING MYTH #1:
One and Done

One and done—or as some call it, "spraying and praying"—is where the salesperson merely makes a bunch of calls that all wind up in voicemail or sends out a ton of emails. In both cases, the salesperson then sits back and *waits* for the phone to ring and orders to come in. Of course nothing happens, and all of the effort that went into making the one round of phone calls winds up being wasted.

The second act of this myth is when the salesperson begins to complain to whoever will listen about how prospecting simply does not work. After telling enough people, the salesperson begins to believe what they've been saying and soon the myth becomes real. To Dennis and his sales team, the myth that prospecting doesn't work was real because they had allowed themselves to believe it. The outcome with Dennis and his team was just as you might imagine—they lost their biggest account, and within sixty days, all of them were out of work.

I'll Prospect When I'm Done Taking Care of My Existing Customers

Salespeople with established accounts hold this myth in high regard. These salespeople know they should be prospecting, but to them prospecting is clearly way down on the list of priorities. Their top objective is ensuring they properly take care of their existing accounts. The truth is the accounts are their top priority because they don't want to have to prospect. They likely view prospecting as something only the new salespeople need to do. To help everything look good, they will even go as far as to tell others that they would love to prospect, but the demands of serving their existing accounts simply doesn't allow any time for prospecting.

It's Impossible to Have a Dedicated Time to Prospect

Salespeople of all types live out this myth daily. The argument is there are so many things going on, and there is little consistency to the day and even the week, that trying to schedule a time to prospect just won't work. This is one myth where management gets involved far too often by making last-minute requests and demands that ultimately require people to change their schedules. Left unchecked, this myth of not being able to schedule time will spill over into other critical activities. Before long, the sales force finds itself in a reactive mode to everything.

We've Made It This Long Without Having to Prospect

This is a myth that will sink companies. A company I worked with early in my consulting career suffered from this myth. When they brought me in the company was barely ten years old, and during that time they had experienced some great growth. The growth had come by having the right relationships at the right time with the right people. Several times throughout the history of the company they had been at a crossroads of not having enough business to remain open, only to suddenly have another major opportunity arise. The entire company believed they could continue to live on this trend of what was nothing more than luck.

This myth may sound like it couldn't happen, but it does—in particular with small companies that grow too quickly and never become adept at understanding how to prospect. This company only survived to twenty years by being part of several mergers to give them the size, stability, and a new sales force that knew how to prospect.

PROSPECTING MYTH #5:

If We Provide Great Customer Service to Our Existing Customers, We Won't Have to Prospect

Customer service is essential, but that in and of itself is rarely going to deliver the new customers necessary to sustain growth or cover for those customers lost due to unforeseen circumstances. It's great to be known for superior customer service, and that and that alone should enthuse you to want to prospect.

PROSPECTING MYTH #6:

Only "Born Salespeople" Can Prospect

This myth simply will not go away. Each time someone quickly finds success in a new sales role, people are quick to say how they're "a born salesperson." It's certainly meant as a compliment to the person, but to others it can come across as a myth being validated. This is especially discouraging to salespeople already struggling to prospect. For them to hear someone is a "born salesperson" proves what they want to believe about why they aren't successful prospecting. They easily assume they can't prospect because they *aren't* "born salespeople."

Being successful at prospecting does not require a set of skills only a few people possess. In the chapters to follow, I will outline the steps you need to not just overcome these prospecting myths, but also to become a top performing salesperson. Prospecting is not an optional activity if you want to be successful. It's an essential one.

CHAPTER 3

Major Factors in Successful Lead Generation

We all know someone who is incredibly brilliant, but in the end doesn't accomplish anything because of a bad attitude. A few years ago, I was asked to work with a team of salespeople at a transportation services company in the Dallas area to help grow their sales, and I quickly encountered this problem in a big way. The sales team at this company was comprised of a cross-section of people, from veterans to new hires, and each one had their own personality and skill set. Before long, I was dealing with one salesperson in particular who was easily the smartest person on the team. His level of knowledge blew me away, and his understanding of the trucking and transportation industries was amazing. If anyone needed a question answered, they went to him.

As smart as this person was, the results he posted each month were near the bottom. The problem became clear to me fairly quickly—he was clearly technically proficient and understood sales well, but his attitude sure did stink! It stunk so much that others were happy when he called in sick. The joke among some of the people on the team was they were hoping something would prevent him from coming to work—or management would wake up and terminate him.

Think about this person for a moment. He was brilliant and had the answers, yet he turned in results that didn't reflect his potential. In the end, his downfall was his attitude and level of motivation. Conversely, there was another person on the team who certainly didn't know the process and was new to sales and the industry. But what he lacked in knowledge and experience, he made up for with an infectious positive attitude and a level of motivation that was at the top of the chart.

Can you relate to the sales team I described? I'm not expecting you to feel you're one of those two personality types, but I'm sure you've seen shades of each in your colleagues. Getting closer to home, I suspect you can find shades of both in your own style.

If you're wondering how the new person with little knowledge and a great attitude did, let me tell you in three words. He crushed it! Yes, he started slow and for the first few months had the worst numbers on the team, but in time he started making his move up the ladder and didn't stop until he was clearly number one in sales. What's more, he didn't occupy the top spot for just a month—he owned it month in and month out! With his infectious attitude, he helped raise everyone's performance, except for one person. Do you know who that was? Yes, you guessed it. It was the man who knew *everything*, but had zero motivation. Did he change? Who knows, but he was given the gift of taking his bad attitude and lack of motivation someplace else, because ultimately he was terminated.

The level of motivation you bring to the task at hand is going to determine the results you achieve. Whenever I'm looking to hire a salesperson, I'll always take attitude over knowledge. Management can teach a person knowledge, but management can't teach a person motivation and attitude. If the potential hire doesn't arrive on the scene with a good attitude, it's doubtful they'll ever have it.

Your Attitude Is Your Problem

Let's get something cleared up right now. Prospecting can be difficult. Why make it any harder by having a bad attitude? Too many salespeople fail to realize how much they're destroying their sales prospecting results due to their attitudes. If you don't think a bad attitude makes a difference, ask yourself how much more you get done in a single day when you have a good attitude versus when you have bad attitude?

My good friend Mike Weinberg, who wrote the introduction for this book, has a great way to help people understand the role attitude plays in sales. In his latest book, *Sales Management. Simplified.* he writes:

> *Sales is a unique type of job. To do it successfully, you have to want to sell. Think about that statement for a minute. A salesperson has to want to sell. There is no way to effectively prospect for new business or penetrate a challenging existing customer if your heart is not in it. A miserable salesperson cannot represent her company, her solution, or herself well. If her heart is not engaged, she won't fight to get in. She won't be able to woo a prospect. She won't go the extra step to ask the hard questions, push past initial resistance, fight back hard against objections, or continue to pursue deals that seem to have gone dark.*
>
> *This may come off as harsh, or even biased, but it's true: a miserable accountant can still do great work. An accountant doesn't require passion to close the books at month-end. An accountant can literally hate her job and yet produce accurate, timely, and valuable financial statements. But good luck trying to find a miserable salesperson who is bringing in new business and delivering her numbers month in and month out. You'll be looking for a long time because she doesn't exist. Miserable, mistreated salespeople don't sell. There are no miserable top performers in sales. Why? Because when their company's anti-sales culture gets out of control, top producers go elsewhere.*

The first thing we have to realize about our attitude? It's up to each of us to determine what our attitude is going to be. Expecting someone to come along each morning and sprinkle "attitude dust" on us to grant us great attitudes is not going to happen. When we allow factors outside of our control to take over our attitudes, we're doomed. There always will be people who will reject your phone calls or make quick off-the-cuff statements about how they feel toward you. The key is to not let these bother you.

Rejection Goes with the Territory

The best example I can share with you of not letting outside factors control you is to think of the late-night hotel front desk clerk. This person is responsible for receiving guests who may have encountered any number of difficulties in their travels to the hotel. The clerk doesn't know any of this, and he or she certainly doesn't have any control over them, yet the guest could still choose to treat the clerk with less than courteous behavior. The guest isn't necessarily doing it intentionally; it's merely the culmination of a difficult day. Same thing goes for the response you may get to your phone call or email. The prospect may simply be responding to you in a manner that reflects other things going on in their life at that moment. Don't let their actions impact your actions. You're better than that, and you probably have not had the same type of day they've had.

View each call you make, email you send, or whatever communication you're using as an opportunity to impact positively the person you're trying to reach. The ability you have to prospect is a privilege, because you are creating opportunity to provide the prospect the same level of service or products you've provided to other customers. Look for the positive, regardless of where it comes from. Use the positive as your springboard to pump your own attitude. This is a key reason I tell outside salespeople who are in their cars to not listen to the talking heads that dominate the airwaves. It's amazing how what you hear, see, and experience quickly winds up impacting your level of motivation.

Would You Buy from Yourself?

I love asking salespeople this question. As much as I want to hear what they say, it's *how* they say it that really tells me something. Typically, salespeople will say they would buy from themselves. Where I find things don't add up is when I compare what they're saying to their tone of voice and body language. Salespeople who are motivated and have a great attitude are able to express without any hesitation with their body language and their tone of voice as to *why* they would buy from themselves. Their voices are enthusiastic and every part of their bodies are revealing the same level of energy.

Now step back and begin to think for a moment about your prospects and customers. What do they *see* in you? If you don't have a strong enough attitude to believe in yourself, why should a prospect believe in you? Salespeople who rely on prospecting or deal primarily with customers where the relationship is a single sale are clearly at a disadvantage if they don't believe in themselves enough to buy from themselves. Your motivation and attitude come from within, and are built on your belief system. This is why I always say a salesperson's greatest asset is their own attitude and personality, and the way they can increase their own success in sales is by building their motivation.

The first step is to realize no one is going to change your attitude or build your level of motivation other than you. It's a decision you have to make and own, one hundred percent. Top performing salespeople and, for that matter, top performers in anything, subscribe to the premise, "It's not anyone's responsibility but my own."

Motivated people exhibit discipline in what they do and how they do it. With regard to prospecting, that means they have established times to prospect in their day and they do it. They don't just *think* about it; they actually do it. This applies also to the process they use. They believe in it, and they have confidence it will create the results they need. Boom! That is the sole reason why I wrote this book and why you're reading it now. I am committed to helping you develop a process that you'll be committed to using.

SEVEN THINGS MOTIVATED PEOPLE DO TO STAY MOTIVATED ➤

1. Motivated people ignore the negative voices in their lives. These might be people in the office and friends who have bad attitudes. They're out there, and if you're not careful, they'll control you, too.
2. Motivated people associate with highly motivated people. Just as there are negative people in the world, there also are positive people. Your job is to make sure you spend as much time with the positive people as possible. This might mean finding

people outside of work because your work environment is full of toxic negativity.

3. Motivated people simply look for the positive in things. Positive people count it an honor to live each day, learn from others, and impact positively those they meet. Positive people take great satisfaction in helping others achieve success.

4. Motivated people don't worry about what they can't control, but are quick to accept control of their worlds. They don't pass the buck to someone else, but are willing to be accountable in everything.

5. Motivated people are continuously learning. They approach each sales call as an opportunity to learn something new, and it's the same approach they take to *everything* they do. The benefit of the learning they do each day is how they use it to improve themselves even more.

6. Motivated people know there will be tough times, but they know tough times don't last. They're aware they need to stay focused on the solution, not the problem. Motivated people always view things in a longer time frame than negative people, who dwell on the negativity of the moment they're in.

7. Motivated people set goals and are focused on achieving them, and along the way they celebrate each positive step. The goals they set are designed to both motivate them and drive them to higher levels of success than others might achieve.

I strongly suggest you take a notebook, and each Friday you record the biggest success you had that week. Then take a moment to celebrate regardless of how small it might seem. After you give yourself a big hug, then record what you want to accomplish the following week. This approach is simple and yet incredibly powerful. Within a few months of doing this each week, you'll see the progress you're making, and what you'll find is your past success will help drive your motivation going forward. I've been sharing this technique for years, and I'm amazed at the comments I get back months and even years later from salespeople who have found the approach to be a huge reason for their success.

In the end, it comes down to one simple belief. If you believe in what you do and realize your job as a salesperson is to help others see and achieve things they didn't think were possible, you'll be amazed at what you can accomplish.

Are You Even Focused?

We've been discussing motivation and attitude, and with those come a level of focus. The easiest way I can tell if someone is motivated is by watching how he or she works. If they're not focused, I'll bet you they're not motivated, and I know I'll be right ninety-eight percent of the time. Being focused and committed comes with the territory for motivated people. Too many salespeople at the first sign of something going wrong get scared and change direction. No wonder so many salespeople cave to the demands of the customer so quickly! The problem is you have to realize there will be obstacles. Things will arise that may give an indication of something not working correctly, but that doesn't mean you should abandon the process.

> ▶ Can you imagine Bill Gates in the early days of Microsoft stopping work just because he encountered a small problem?
> ▶ I wonder if Steve Jobs would have stopped all work on the iPhone just because somebody said something he didn't like.

In both cases, we know that they did not stop. Why, then, should you stop everything and go into panic mode or haphazardly come up with a new process just because a small issue arises? Once you have your sales process established, then stick to it. You have to give it time. If it normally takes you two months to prospect a customer and close the sale, then you want to use your process for at least six months before evaluating it.

You can make tweaks along the way. That's fine, but don't go abandoning the ship halfway across the ocean. The amount of time you need to devote to your prospecting process must be at least three times the length of the normal customer acquisition process. Saying it doesn't work before you've given it enough time will leave you in a continuous state of change. You'll only be in a position to evaluate the effectiveness of a sales process after you've been doing it for an extended period of time. Don't cop out on yourself. I find the reason salespeople are quick to throw up their hands about their prospecting system not working is because they want to have an excuse to not have to prospect.

It's User Error, Not System Error

Far more prospecting systems fail due to user error than due to system error. This message applies not only to salespeople, but also to sales managers, the marketing department, and anyone else involved in the sales process. Things take time. A new customer is not going to suddenly pop out of thin air based on one phone call or one email. If prospecting were that easy, we wouldn't need salespeople.

In prospecting, the key is to avoid becoming discouraged when something doesn't go right. You must be able to withstand being rejected time and time again. Keep in mind that if prospecting were easy, your potential to make big bucks would not exist—somebody would have created an app to do it instead. The reason sales can be such a profitable profession is due to the reality that many people cannot survive the rejection in this profession and aren't willing to stay focused.

The top salespeople with whom I have the privilege to interact have high levels of focus and drive. I see it exhibited in them by the way they refuse to let a comment from a customer or even a string of bad events from a number of customers or prospects dampen their enthusiasm for finding the next sale. These high achievers not only have the attitude to keep going on sales call after sales call, but they also are able *within* calls to keep things moving forward. When most salespeople would say a sales call is over and there is little potential to secure a sale, the high performer is able to ask just the right question or make the right comment to re-engage the customer.

Are these people successful every time? Of course not. But over a period of time, they will put together enough wins to come out on top. Focus and commitment come from within. It's the personal drive that moves you forward when everything else is saying stop. The comparison I like to use is running a marathon. It doesn't take much to *start* a marathon, but it takes a runner with commitment to *finish* a marathon.

Running a marathon is as much mental as it is physical, and many would say that a marathon is started with the legs, but finished with the mind. If you fail to believe mentally, there is no way the physical effort will carry you through. Same thing in sales—you may know the process and you may know your product, but if you don't know yourself, you won't be successful. Your attitude is the difference.

PART II

PREPARING FOR PROSPECTING SUCCESS

4

Planning for High-Profit Customers

The definition of insanity is continuing to do the same thing over and over and expecting a different result. Unfortunately, this exemplifies the expectations of too many sales prospecting plans. At one time I could have put myself in this same camp. When I decided to leave my corporate job and the corner office that came with it in October 1998 to open my new consulting business, I felt I could deal with any sales issue quickly and in the right way. I thought the key to success was going to be doing for myself what I used to do for the companies where I had been so successful. How could I possibly go wrong? At least, that's what I thought.

Over the years, I had held prominent sales positions in several major corporations, and over that time I had the ability to sell to other equally large companies. My personal belief system was built on the premise that I had been with the best companies, selling to the best customers, and that meant I was one of the best. My mistake was trying to use the same sales and prospecting process that had worked for me at my prior companies with my new consulting company. Despite my sense that my prospecting process wasn't working, I was far too hesitant to change. I assumed that if I just pushed hard enough, worked long enough, and remained focused on my objectives, I would be successful. Go ahead and say it—*I* was the definition of insanity. Finally, after pain, anguish, grief, stress, and everything else you want to throw into the mix, I realized I needed to change how I prospected if I was going to expect my company to succeed.

Far too many salespeople never take a big enough step back from their businesses to realize what they need to change. This is why I'm a big proponent of always watching other industries beyond the one in which you work. When we only look within, we are far too likely to merely repeat the same thing over and over again. Insanity comes at us from many directions, but one example I see far too often is when sales teams and companies fail to bring successful ideas from other industries into their worlds. After eighteen months trying to make things happen in my new company, I realized the changes I needed to make were going to come from areas where I had never thought to look. The decision I had to make was if I was going to be content with low expectations, or if I was going to challenge the status quo to find a better way?

Prospects Don't Want Average

This is where accepting average as being *just fine* winds up destroying far too many salespeople and companies. Average is not something anyone should aspire to. Why reside at *average*? Doing so creates an open invitation for your competitor to steal your business. Prospects aren't looking for average. They're looking to excel, and the only salespeople with whom they want to work are ones who share the same drive. Failing to question every aspect of what you do, look beyond your industry, and challenge the process is saying you're willing to be just average. Being average isn't going to get you the customers you really need, and it's not going to allow you to achieve the level of success you know you're capable of.

On the following pages are critical questions. My goal is to challenge your thinking and ultimately allow you to develop a baseline of where you are today and a vision of where you need to go. Over the years, I've had the privilege to work with thousands of salespeople in numerous industries and all sizes and types of organizations focused on both B2B and B2C. During this time, I've developed a robust set of questions to evaluate their current state of affairs. If you want to change, you need to know your base.

These are the same questions I ask companies that hire me as a consultant. In working through these questions with companies and salespeople, I've never found a situation where an organization or salesperson isn't doing at least some things well. Use the questions to guide your understanding of what's working and what's not working. Don't rush through them! You may choose to only *read* the questions now, so you can continue reading the rest of the book. That's fine. Just don't forget to come back and spend the time you need coming up with solid answers.

I've broken the questions into two sets. The first set is more strategic in nature: these will challenge how you see yourself and how your customers see you. Answers to these will be more thought-based; but remember, in the end, it's not what *you* think that is vital, but rather it's what your customers think. The second set of questions is tactical in scope to help you better understand your process and its effectiveness.

Seven Strategic Questions Regarding Your Prospecting Process

1. **What about my prospecting process is compelling to the customer?**

   When I say "compelling," I am talking about the customer's willingness to engage and share with you what they truly want. Prospects won't do that unless they find you and your process compelling and full of potential to help them meet their needs.

2. **Does my prospecting process result in the customer having false expectations about what I sell, and thus force me to spend time later in the selling process reshaping them?**

   Nothing can suck more profit out of a company than having customers demanding something they feel they deserve based on comments made by a salesperson.

3. **Is my prospecting process effective enough to help reduce the amount of time I spend negotiating with customers?**

   The better we prospect with regard to finding and validating great potential customers, the less negotiating we will have to do to close a sale.

4. **Is my prospecting process focused more on sharing with the customer what I have to offer or is it more about uncovering information about the customer?**

   Prospecting processes that do not put learning about the customer first are only going to result in a high level of "no" answers from customers. There is no way you can be successful with your prospecting if you're chasing leads that don't have potential.

5. **Is my prospecting process segmented enough to allow me to uncover customer needs faster from different types of prospects than if I used the same process for everyone?**

   Not all prospects are the same. They may have the same buying profile, but their communication needs may be polar opposites. The sooner you can tailor *how* you prospect, the greater the number of customers you will close.

6. **How does the customer see me and how I can help them?**

   The number and different types of questions prospects ask you during the selling process is going to help you understand how well they see you and what you sell.

7. **How long does it take for a lead or prospect to have confidence in me?**

   Prospecting is all about building confidence. The sooner the customer has confidence in you, the sooner you'll be able to accurately uncover their needs.

Thirty Tactical Questions to Measure Your Effectiveness and Process

I designed these thirty questions to help you start pulling apart the individual components of what you're doing now to prospect.

1. Where do your sales leads come from? List by type and percentage. Examples: referral, website, cold calling, marketing, etc.
2. What percentage of each type of lead do you ultimately close?

3. How many sales calls does it take to close each sale? Break this list down by type to include phone call, voicemail, live meeting, email, etc.

4. How long does it take to close a sale from the time the lead first develops? Break these down by source: referral, networking, cold calling, etc.

5. By customer type, list the key reasons each customer tells you why they buy from you.

6. By customer type, list the key reasons each customer tells you why they are not going to buy from you.

7. How much time do you spend each day/week in the actual activity of interacting with prospects?

8. How much time do you spend in activities preparing to prospect? Break these activities down into specific categories with the amount of time spent on each.

9. What percentage of your new customers becomes repeat customers?

10. How much is a new customer worth to you in gross sales and net profit in the first year? What type of customer is your most profitable? What type is the least profitable?

11. Is there a particular product or service new customers are drawn to? Does this vary by type of lead?

12. Is there a time of year when prospects are more inclined to make a decision or avoid making a decision?

13. What is the average transaction amount for a new customer?

14. What is the profit from an average transaction for a new customer?

15. What is the three-year value of each new customer in revenue and profit?

16. Does the customer have to buy, or is what they're buying purely discretionary?

17. What are the customer's options should they decide not to buy from you?

18. Is every new customer for you a lost customer for someone else?

19. Is the customer's buying decision of critical importance to them?

20. What percentage of your prospects comes to you via referrals?
21. What is the close ratio of those who come to you via referral?
22. What percentage of your customers is experiencing your product/industry for the first time?
23. How much of a financial impact does buying from you have on the customer? Consider this with regard to cash flow, flexible resources, etc.
24. Is the customer's buying decision geared toward preventing a problem or enhancing an opportunity?
25. When does the prospect first bring up the cost to buy?
26. How long does the average customer remain your customer?
27. Do the majority of your new customers buy a similar item/service from you again? How long until they do so?
28. What is the "after purchase" relationship like with the customer?
29. How knowledgeable is the average prospect about your industry and what you sell when you first make contact with them?
30. How well can you profile your typical customer, and does this allow you to know better how to target them?

Notice there's not one question asked about the type of Customer Relationship Management (CRM) system you use. This is intentional, as I strongly believe too many salespeople are quick to blame any short-comings in their prospecting processes on the CRM system they're either using or not using. Sorry, that's not the case in 98 percent of all situations. Do I believe you need to have a CRM system? Yes, I absolutely do, but remember that the CRM system is a tool to *help* you do your job, not a tool that does your job for you.

Use the questions I've listed as a directional guide to help you begin to determine how you need to alter your sales prospecting plan. I ask clients after they answer these questions to go back over them and look for areas that stand out as opportunities for improvement. It might surprise you, but after having a salesperson or sales team answer these questions, I've yet to have anyone come back without at least one or two areas where they see room for improvement. Having the answers to these questions and a sense of which areas you need to develop will help you gain even more value from the rest of this book.

CHAPTER 5

Fit the Prospecting Plan to Your Market

I regularly receive emails and phone calls from salespeople looking for quick advice on how to prospect better. One particular email that stood out was from a salesperson with a new European-based company providing services in the general aviation industry. For those not familiar with this industry, it is made up of everything that flies, excluding the airlines. Since I've worked a lot in this industry, I quickly had interest in the email. The person sending it wanted me to evaluate the prospecting plan his company was using, as he was continually falling short of meeting his numbers. He emailed me a summary of the plan he had been following. It became clear I needed to speak with him, as I was shocked by what I saw.

The plan consisted of identifying anyone in the general aviation industry, calling them, telling them everything the company could offer, and asking for the order. The problem? Nobody in the industry needed what the company had to offer because they already had somebody providing it for them. When building the business plan, the owners of the company thought customers would switch to them immediately if asked.

If you operated a small jet, where safety is the first thing you think about each day, would you give business to a brand new company just because they called you? No! There is no way you would move from an established relationship with a vendor that was already delivering the service you expected.

During my conversations with the salesperson, it became evident that in his desperation to find business he would share in his phone calls and emails a laundry list of services his company could provide. The more desperate he became, the longer the list he would share. This was only making a bad problem even worse. It came down to three things: One, he didn't know who the ultimate decision maker was; two, he didn't understand the customer's needs; and three, he didn't have a plan to establish confidence.

This will help you save huge amounts of time—and ultimately make you huge amounts of money. You will learn how to avoid being the salesperson I just described. You may say that you're not like that salesperson and your company would never take that approach. Sure, the situation I shared is extreme, but don't think for a moment you or your company don't have areas that need improvement. (Maybe the title of this chapter should be changed to "How to Save Time and Make More Money.") Prospecting requires having a process. Even more important than having a process, it's having one that fits you and your market.

What Are You Selling? Who Are You Selling It To?

Here are seven questions you need to answer before building your prospecting plan:

1. Do I sell a consumable or something people buy on a regular basis?
2. Is what I sell considered a routine purchase or is it a capital expenditure/major expense?
3. Are my customers professional buyers who interface with numerous salespeople?
4. If the customer chooses not to buy from me, are they buying from my competitor, or not making a purchase at all?
5. Are my prospects currently buying what I sell from someone else?
6. Is what I sell purchased via a contract, quote, or some other type of deadline process?

7. Are customers familiar with what I sell or is it something I
   need to educate them about?

Let's go through these seven questions in greater detail and look at
what they mean.

1. Do I sell a consumable or something people buy on a regular basis?

If the customer is buying on a regular basis, it means the frequency with which we should be reaching out to the lead or prospect
could be as often as several times a week. B2B Example: If you're
selling building supplies, your prospects may easily be making buying
decisions daily, so contacting them two, three, or even four times per
week may not be excessive at all.

Conversely, if you're selling something customers buy on an
annual basis only, your frequency of contact may need to be only
every three to four weeks. B2C Example: If you sell pest control services to homeowners and it's typically an annual contract, contacting
them monthly would be appropriate.

2. Is what I sell considered a routine purchase or is it a capital expenditure/major expense?

Items that are considered a routine purchase will typically not
need as much of an approval process for a customer to buy. This
most likely will mean the person responsible for buying might be
lower in an organization.

If, on the other hand, what you're selling is considered a capital
expenditure, it can mean going through multiple decision makers
to gain a sale. You may need to build your prospecting strategy
around multiple prospects in the same company. Additionally, if it's
a capital expenditure it most likely means it is in the annual plan,
which may lengthen the prospecting process to months rather than
weeks.

A person selling life insurance or other financial services may find
the decision-making process involves two people and can extend
over several months or even longer, because the customer places a
great weight on making a right decision for two people, rather than
just one.

3. **Are my customers professional buyers who interface with numerous salespeople?**

   If you're prospecting professional buyers, you're dealing with people who know how to take advantage of salespeople. This means they will most likely subscribe to the practice of never acknowledging your prospecting efforts until they are at the point of making a buying decision. Their silence doesn't mean you don't prospect to them. No, it means consistency is key, because professional buyers don't want to work with people in whom they have no confidence. Few prospecting activities will build more confidence than consistency.

4. **If the customer chooses not to buy from me, are they buying from my competitor, or not making a purchase at all?**

   If the prospect is clearly buying either from you *or* your competitor, it means your prospecting process must be frequent enough to allow you to be on the front end of the buying process. This means you must place a strong emphasis on developing relationships over a period of time and educating customers along the way.

5. **Are my prospects currently buying what I sell from someone else?**

   This is typically the hardest type of lead. With the lead already buying from someone else, it means your prospecting efforts are geared toward creating awareness. Short of having a significant point of difference, you're typically waiting for the incumbent to stumble. The upside is when you're successful gaining this customer, they most likely become a loyal, long-term customer.

   Don't view these types of customers as not being worthy of your prospecting time. Invariably, the competitor that currently has the account will at some point make a mistake or have an issue. If you have taken the time to build awareness, you could be the one the customer turns to when the existing supplier slips up.

6. **Is what I sell purchased via a contract, quote, or some other type of deadline process?**

   I can't emphasize enough the need to be careful if you sell into this space. Customers who use this approach will actively engage with multiple companies at the same time, only to play the companies against each other. Too many salespeople don't understand this. As such, they will have what they think is a great pipeline, only to have it go bust time and time again. These customers also require long lead times (maybe even as much as several years) due to the length of some contracts.

Your prospecting efforts here must be two-fold. First, you want to find out their timeline, and second, you want to build your credibility. Your sole objective is to be on the front end of the process and not be the one invited to the party at the last minute. Ultimately, your prospecting is going be over a long period of time with multiple contacts in the same organization.

7. **Are customers familiar with what I sell or is it something I need to educate them about?**

If the people to whom you're talking are not familiar with how you can help them, your prospecting process must include enough time and communication to allow the customer to become educated.

An example is when Apple rolled out its first smartphone. People who were sold on the Apple ecosystem were quick to adopt the phone, but for many people there was hesitancy because they didn't know how a smartphone could help them.

What do the answers to these questions mean? They mean the process you develop must fit your market. Don't think you can copy what somebody else does. I designed this book to give you the insights and guidance to help you build a plan that best suits your goals.

Even after you've developed a master process, keep in mind there still will be variations. You'll find yourself with results far less lucrative than what they could or should be. Yes, it will take more time to break your method apart depending on the specific type of customer, but it will yield more success. Use the questions laid out in chapter 4 to help you determine where you need these variations.

Tailor Your Plan for Each Prospect

Just as I'm keen on every sales team and even every salesperson having a tailored prospecting plan to fit broad customer types, I am also keen on having a tailored plan for each individual prospect. It's no different than fixing something around your home. You can't use the same tool to fix everything; there are certain tools for certain jobs. For example, you're not going to reach a senior-level manager using the same process you would to reach a low-level person. Segment your prospects by the type of message and strategy that will most likely engage them. A low-level person is far more likely to take a phone call than a senior-level person who isn't going to talk with anyone they don't trust.

The message and strategy also will have different timelines associated with them. Your prospecting timelines and the frequency of the messages are going to vary by whom you're trying to reach. Another example I use is if you're selling into the educational market, trying to reach a professor at the start of the academic year is simply not going to work. Conversely, if you're trying to reach a graduate student, the start of the academic year might be perfect.

Frequency also is going to vary. A simple rule I like to follow: the higher up in an organization the person is or the more knowledgeable they are, the less frequent my contacts will be. The lower a person is, the more frequently I can contact them.

The higher up in an organization a person is, the more I will be running into gatekeepers and the more likely I may be able to reach them using contacts with whom they are already comfortable. Lower in an organization, the more it can be a game of simply being there to get noticed.

This issue comes up a lot in conversations I have with people, including my good friend and a person with whom I often work, Anthony Iannarino (www.thesalesblog.com/). Anthony has a great perspective on the issue of tailoring your message. Here's what he has to say:

Not all clients are created equal. Neither are all prospects. It's easy to spend your time with prospects who are receptive, who are willing to meet with you. But the real results you need in sales only come from pursuing your "dream clients," those prospects for whom you can create breath-taking, jaw-dropping, earth-shattering value.

Your "dream clients" allow you to build real, sustainable results. You will never win these clients if you don't start spending time working on them now. They aren't easy to win, and it takes time. But it's what produces outsized results.

One Size Does Not Fit All

Your objective is to tailor your prospecting process based on the type of prospect and to know that the frequency, timing, message, and delivery process will be different. This ties back into the first item on the list. You must be able to segment, and don't think for a moment it's around what you sell.

Segmenting is about whom the prospect is and the outcomes they expect to achieve. For example, one type of prospect might consider your offer a way of preventing pain or risk in their business. Another person may look at the same item you sell as a way to gain a competitive advantage. What this means is your approach and messaging must be different for each prospect. What works for one is not going to work for the other.

Frequently, you are not going to know the specific needs of your prospects until you meet with them. This means you might have to vary your prospecting process after the first contact. For example, you might be selling software, and your target buyers are finance departments. The person buying the software to prevent risk is most likely driven by a different timetable than the person buying it as a competitive advantage. The sooner you identify these needs, the sooner you can tailor your approach.

We see this many times in the home improvement industry. The salesperson is selling to one spouse who may assume the role of decision maker, and the whole time the other spouse is the one setting the expectations. The challenge is that many times prospects may look alike to you on the surface, and it's only after you've had a first contact that you then know which way to lead. This is why it's so important to build your prospecting process around gaining information.

The best way to do this is by asking questions or posing scenarios designed to allow the prospect to share their true need. Your objective is to review why customers have bought from you in the past, and use this knowledge to build out options you can use going forward. In later chapters, we will dive deep into the topic of questions and how to use different types of questions, depending on the situation, to get the best outcomes for you and the customer.

PART III

TIPS, TOOLS, AND TECHNIQUES

CHAPTER 6

Time-Management Tactics

E arly in my consulting career, I was working with a company known for employing creative geniuses who designed for the consumer goods industry. After each time I was with them, I left in amazement at the ideas they created for their clients and the fun they had doing it. The salespeople were all long-term veterans of the industry, and their role as account managers was to maintain enough projects coming to keep the creative team busy.

The CEO brought me in to help them do two things—stabilize their business and open up new business segments around which they could build a new division. The biggest problem I saw was *when* and *how* they prospected. They had the faulty philosophy that they only needed to prospect when business was slow. In the mind of the vice president of sales, prospecting was drudgery and it didn't fit the fun, creative environment they had, so he didn't want to require anyone in the company to do it. He also felt making people prospect was not the right way to treat a veteran sales team. Therefore, whenever the company found itself in a slump, his solution would be to get everyone on the phone calling prospects in what he would call a "prospecting telethon."

In theory, the strategy of a "prospecting telethon" isn't horrible, but what made it bad in this case was there was zero—and I mean *zero*—follow-through on the leads generated from the blitz. Almost by magic, a day or two following a blitz, some massive piece of business would fall out of the sky. Then, the vice president of sales would feel good about things, and the leads generated from the prospecting blitz would fade into the sunset. The salespeople simply would go about doing what they wanted to do, taking care of existing clients, and completely ignoring what needed to be done to develop new business. The result was as you might guess. Six to nine months later, the vice president of sales would declare the sky was falling and he would schedule a "prospecting telethon."

In my conversations with each account manager, their response to my question about why they didn't follow up on leads from the phone blitzes was always the same. Each one said it was impossible to find the time, as they were already overloaded taking care of existing business. Were they *too* busy? No, they weren't any busier than any other account manager for any other company. In reality, they were too busy because they told themselves they were too busy—so often, in fact, they began to believe it. Their reason for saying they were too busy was because they didn't want to endure what they felt was work that was beneath what should be expected of a veteran salesperson.

Prospecting Is Not the Last Thing on Your To-Do List

Prospecting is not something you do when you don't have anything else to do. It's not something you do when you suddenly find yourself without enough customers. Prospecting must be something you do on a regular basis. View prospecting the same way you do taking a shower. You take a shower daily, and you should be prospecting daily. Failing to prospect on a regular basis is putting yourself in a situation where your sales will constantly be in a peak/valley syndrome.

Even if you are extremely successful, or don't feel there is a need to prospect because your customers like you so much, the truth is you *must* prospect consistently! You must allocate time on your calendar—and this doesn't mean just adding it to your list of things you *want* to get done. No, you must physically block the time on your calendar. Minimally, block time each week. Ideally, block time every day. Dedicated time built into your day will increase your probability of doing it. For too many salespeople, prospecting is the last thing they want to do because of how difficult it can be. Merely having it on your list of things to do is simply not good enough.

Time for Prospecting Means You Actually Prospect

The next step in allocating time to prospect is actually doing it. Thinking about prospecting and preparing to prospect is *not* prospecting. Too many salespeople will have an hour of time blocked on their calendars, only to spend the entire hour getting ready to prospect, but never actually doing it. When you allocate time, include time for preparation. For most salespeople, this means setting aside twice as much time as they think they will need. When I'm asked how much time salespeople should spend prospecting, I say divide your calendar into fourths. If you work a forty-hour week, you have four quarters each week containing ten hours each. Allocate the quarters as follows:

Prospecting. Developing leads and qualifying prospects

Existing Accounts. Connecting with your existing customers

Sales Calls/Proposals. Making calls on prospects in the middle of the sales funnel, the high-potential prospects, and customers with whom you're trying to close more deals

Customer Follow-Up/Admin. Taking care of customer issues, attending sales meetings, and completing administrative work

Don't tell me you don't need to dedicate 25% of your time to prospecting. Prospecting is what keeps your sales engine going. Prospect today and you will have leads to work tomorrow, and leads tomorrow mean you have people to sell to next week. When you have people to sell to next week, you have the ability to close deals and make money. It's not a matter of how much time should you prospect; it's a question of how much success you want!

Does Your Clock Match Your Prospect's Clock?

Ask yourself the following questions when you set aside a time period to make prospecting calls: First, is it a time when the decision makers are most likely available? Second, is it a time when you're mentally prepared? Sometimes these two periods conflict with one another, and if they do, then I guarantee it will create a problem. The solution is simple. When your pipeline is empty and you're not making enough money, you'll begin to change your view. You will become more discerning about mentally preparing yourself and making calls when prospects are most likely available. The exact day or days of the week and times of the day you set aside for making prospecting calls will vary based on whom and where you're calling. In chapter 11, I will discuss how to best determine days and times that will work best for your situation.

Your challenge is to maximize the window by being mentally prepared to call. You *must* be prepared. If you merely go into your daily "prospect-calling window" cold, I guarantee your success rate will be zero.

Don't Start What You Can't Finish

I cannot emphasize enough that prospecting is not about the initial calls; it's about the consistency of the calls. A huge mistake people make when prospecting is thinking they're being efficient by making a bunch of calls or emailing a group of prospects *once*. The definition of prospecting is creating a level of awareness with those who might do business with you. You can't accomplish that goal with a single phone call or email.

Before starting to prospect, you must first ask yourself if you have the time and ability to make the necessary number of follow-up contacts with the people you intend to prospect. Just answering this question truthfully can and will save you a tremendous amount of time. To put it bluntly, you are not being productive in your prospecting efforts if you don't have an effective process for following up. I am a huge advocate of having dedicated blocks of time on your calendar to which you adhere. I knew one sales manager who would routinely schedule sales meetings on the best prospecting day of the week.

When I challenged him, he said he was trying to make it easy because that was the one day each week he knew all his salespeople would be in the office. He was making it easy all right—for his sales team to have an excuse to not prospect and then an excuse as to why they couldn't make their numbers.

CHAPTER 7

Are You Prospecting or Wasting Your Time?

The problem is too many salespeople spend time doing things they think are going to bring them prospects, when in reality all they're doing is wasting time. For example, many salespeople can spend a ton of time networking with people who have zero potential of ever being a customer. They may even know there is zero potential, but they network with them anyway, thinking somehow these people are going to magically give them amazing referrals.

Counterintuitive Lead Generation

If you think finding leads is the responsibility of the marketing department and you don't need to worry about it, do me a favor. Stop reading—not only this chapter, but also the rest of the book. Yes, a key part of marketing's job is to find leads for sales, but sales also plays a crucial role in finding leads. I have yet to meet a top-performing salesperson who does not believe it is his or her responsibility to develop leads. Sure, they'll take whatever marketing gives them, but they know the best leads and prospects will be the ones they find and cultivate themselves.

Before we go any further, let's clearly define some key prospecting terms:

Leads—the names and contact information of people who you feel could be viable customers for your business. They may come to you as an inbound lead from marketing or, as I prefer, from activities you're doing.

Prospects—people who you feel are qualified to one degree or another to become customers at some point. The most likely way they become prospects is due to the dialogue you've had with them.

Customers—people who are either already buying from you or are well-developed prospects with whom you are close to securing an order.

Depending on your industry, there can be slight variances with the definitions, but for the purposes of this book and our discussions going forward, this is how I will define these three groups.

A few years ago, a major automobile manufacturer hired me to help them develop a lead-generating program for their salespeople to use in all of their dealerships. Think about that task for a moment and what it says about the millions of dollars spent on ad campaigns and marketing programs used to attract customers. Even with all of the money the manufacturer was spending, they still weren't reaching their potential. They felt (and their research confirmed) that advertising and marketing can do a great job of creating awareness and will drive *some* people to buy, but not enough people. Their ad agencies felt the best way to generate an even higher return on their ad budgets would be to use salespeople as part of the lead generation process.

As a salesperson, you want a strong marketing department. From my own experience as a salesperson, it was a lot easier to develop new business when marketing was doing their job, and doing it well. Marketing's job is to create awareness and help develop leads, but top-performing salespeople in any industry know they also have to be prospecting.

The challenge is *where* to find the leads and, more importantly, *how* to make sure the leads you generate are good. The next chapter deals with qualifying leads. This is devoted to where to find them.

Who You Prospect Will Determine the Price You Get

Before we jump into discussing where to find leads, let's get something basic (yet misunderstood) on the table right now. The type of leads you get will determine the price you get. The example I share whenever I'm speaking on this subject is, "You can't take a Walmart shopper and make them a Nordstrom customer." Walmart shoppers are price driven, while a Nordstrom customer is driven by fashion. Yes, both retailers would say much more than just that about their target markets, but I'm trying to keep this simple.

If you're not getting the price you want, you might need to analyze more than just your selling process. The problem might be your prospecting process and specifically *whom* you're targeting in that process. The price you get when you close the sale starts with the person at the top of your sales funnel. In B2B selling, this may mean you are targeting the right company, but not the right person.

Prospecting is not about going after whoever will talk with you or whoever you get routed to the first time you break through in the company you're trying to reach. Prospecting is about focusing your efforts toward the person(s) with the greatest potential to deliver not just a sale, but also a sale at maximum price. The easiest guideline to follow is to remember buyers who buy based on *tactical* reasons tend to be economic buyers. Buyers who buy based on *strategic* needs are solution buyers. Solution buyers always will provide you with a better opportunity to maximize price. What does all this mean to you in the prospecting process? It means a lot.

The key is to determine early on why the prospect is willing to talk with you. If the prospect is not willing to share with you their strategic issues, then you're not at the right level of the organization. Don't fall for the idea that just because you're talking with the "user" or "owner" of what you're selling that you can maximize price. Many "users" are so low in the organization that they have zero control over budget, meaning even though they might be a "user," they're really nothing more than an economic buyer. If you sell baby furniture, you know the baby is the user of the furniture, but they're certainly not the decision maker.

"Users" still can be a source of valuable information to you, but the person with whom you really want to enter into a sales conversation and identify as the potential prospect is the one who recognizes what you offer is a *strategic* benefit. Find the strategic-oriented prospect and you'll find less pressure to discount your price when you close the sale.

We will dig into these issues more in the chapters to come, but in the meantime, I want you to always remember it's not just about developing leads, but rather it's about developing *good* leads you can convert into long-term customers.

Love the Ones You're With

Never waste an opportunity to ask a current customer who else might benefit from what you sell. The key to turn these new leads into great leads is to ask the customer giving you the lead to introduce you to the new prospect.

A good friend of mine, Bill Cates, has made it his mission in life to show people how to get leads. His approach: ask a customer for a lead any time you have delivered value. He is so well respected he is called the "Referral Coach." (Check him out at www.referralcoach. com/.) Few salespeople go this far when working with referrals, but those who do are top performers. After the customer has given you a name, ask the customer if they would be so kind as to introduce you to the person via email, telephone, or whatever other means possible. I'll discuss this later on in chapter 16, which is devoted exclusively to the art of referrals.

Hug Your Competitor's Customers

The reason these companies are not only just a lead, but also a great prospect, is because they're already sold on what you sell. The only problem is they're buying it from someone else. Engage with these people frequently. When the other person fails to deliver, you will be first in the customer's mind as someone to call for help.

The thrill of picking up a new customer this way is incredible. To me, this approach is by far the easiest way to generate prospects because you don't have to educate them—too many salespeople lose way too much time prospecting because the only leads they're going after are ones they have to educate.

The number of salespeople who are afraid to use this approach surprises me. Not surprisingly, these are the same salespeople who continually struggle to make their numbers. Just keep in mind that if you're doing it to your competitors, then if they're smart, they're doing it to you. Get the drift? The best way to keep a customer is to make sure you're taking care of them.

Fill the Bus You're Driving

Every organization has turnover—these days, people are constantly moving from one company to another. A great way to pick up a new customer is by having someone familiar with what you do take you with them to their new employer. Your existing customers also may have other divisions, operating units, etc. Again, this is an incredibly easy way to pick up new leads. I always aim to take the easiest approach possible, and I don't care where I get the leads or business.

An easy way to gain additional leads from existing customers is to monitor closely who is copied on emails you receive from the company. Each name on the "cc" list is worthy of contacting. Even if you do this for no other reason than to better understand the business, it's a good idea. It's a bonus if you uncover new opportunities. The same goes for when you send an email to someone and you receive an automated reply stating they're out of the office or unavailable. Often these reply emails include the name and phone number of who to contact if necessary. Guess what? It's necessary! Contact them!

"Secret Societies" Don't Have to Be Secret

The amount of business you can pick up from knowing how to leverage industry trade associations is amazing. I worked with one salesperson who, when she started out, focused exclusively on developing leads— and ultimately customers—from industry trade associations. Before long, she had a full pipeline and was making her sales goals.

Your first step when exploring trade associations or industries is to visit their websites and see if they have their membership rosters online. It may surprise you, but a number of groups do make their membership lists available. If that's the case, go for it. Even more powerful than a membership roster is the list of members who are on the board or serve on a special committee.

These people are engaged and passionate about their industry, otherwise they wouldn't serve their peers by being active in their trade association. This makes these people valuable not just as leads, but also as sources of great knowledge. These folks also are the ones other people in the association come to for advice. What better way to develop even more leads than by serving a board member well and having them refer you to others!

If you're wondering how to reach out to these people, it's simple. First approach is with a phone call. You merely state you found their names on the association website and you have a few questions about the industry. The key is to be legit! Don't go blowing smoke. Remember, you're looking for insights to help you better understand their industry so you can ultimately serve them better.

Use email if you can't connect on the telephone, and place the name of the association in the subject line. They'll spot the association name and likely take the time to read it. Your email should then contain the same questions you would have asked if you were speaking with them on the telephone.

Another approach with associations is to reach out to the staff of these organizations. Many times, the larger ones will have multiple people on staff. Ideally, contact the person in charge of membership. This person is gold—they're talking with members all the time, and as a result, are going to know better than anyone what's happening out there. It's like getting an industry education for free!

Don't Forget Your "Exes"

If I had a dollar for each blank stare I've received from salespeople when I shared the idea of reaching out to old customers, I'd be retired. The response I get after sharing this idea is something like, "I'm not going to do that! We really did some stupid stuff with them and I know they don't like us." How do you know how the customer feels? How do you know what they'll say? You won't know until you make the call. More often than not, the customer has long forgotten the mistake you thought was so fatal. If you don't take the time to reach out and call every old customer who is no longer buying from you, you're overlooking huge opportunities to build your business quickly. And if the customer does remember the poor job your company did, don't you want a shot at correcting it? Sure you do! If you fail to correct it, you run the risk of the customer telling others about the problem, making your job even harder.

Contacting old customers is something I stress new hires should do immediately, because they can make the calls without any implication of being "part of the problem" should a customer bring it up. As the new person, you are reaching out because you're eager to help and eager to show them the quality work your company can do.

Another great benefit of having a new person call all the old customers—it's a great way for them to become educated on the company and the industry. I've found during the course of making these calls to old customers, many will share insights with the new person. What a great way for a new salesperson to get educated by making prospecting phone calls!

Years ago, a company called and asked to use my services to evaluate their salespeople. The objective was to find out what makes the top performers the top performers, and then see if the company could replicate those qualities in other salespeople. The first task I did was to look at the numbers each salesperson was turning in and compare those to their time in their position and the current market.

One person's numbers jumped out to me immediately. She was a recent hire who was right out of college and she had zero industry experience. In less than six months, she had moved from the bottom of the list to the middle of the list and was trending to go even higher.

I immediately contacted her to find out what she had done. After getting over the shock of me calling (and thinking she had done something wrong), she explained she had just done what her boss had told her—contacted a massive list of old customers that past salespeople had walked away from or the company had let slide away. All she did was call each one and from there, poof! The business began flowing!

A "No" Is Never Permanent

Just because they chose not to buy from you once doesn't mean they won't buy from you now. A "no" from a prospect is never permanent; a "no" is only a period of time. Reach out and contact them again. Don't let whatever you heard a year ago, a month ago, or even a week ago stop you. What happened yesterday is not an indicator of what might happen today. It's amazing the number of professional buyers and purchasing agents who tell me that too many salespeople go silent on them after losing an order to a competitor or a decision not to buy. To me this puts a bad stain on the sales community. It makes it look like all we're about is a quick sale, and if we don't get our way, we run home to mommy and pout. You might have not received the order yesterday, but that is no reason to stop reaching out. Be professional and have confidence you have something of value that can help the customer. The only way they can see how much you can help them is if you convince them to buy from you.

Find New Dance Partners

I'm not saying to dance with your immediate competitor, but without a doubt there are salespeople in your industry who sell things that you do not. So, it only makes sense to help each other out. Develop relationships with them, because not only are you looking for potential customers, but they are too. Share names and insights so you both succeed.

One trick I like sharing with salespeople is a method to use if they're consistently unable to get past the switchboard. If you have a situation like this, listen to the prompts and press the appropriate number to connect with the sales department. I love this approach, because the salesperson who answers is typically going to be a junior salesperson, somebody new to the company likely trying to build their sales, too. Introduce yourself as a fellow salesperson and tell them whom you're trying to reach. You'll be amazed at how quickly most salespeople will help you because you are another salesperson. Go one step further and ask if they will connect you right then on the phone with a personal introduction.

Over the years, I've shared this approach with thousands of sales-people, and each time I am met with shock at how simple the idea is. Occasionally, I receive a call back a week or so later from a salesperson saying how they used it and it worked beautifully. Remember, just as you were looking for assistance with a lead, the salesperson who helps you also is looking for leads. Don't end the conversation without trying to help them in their jobs.

Know Your Purchasing Department

Get in touch with your purchasing department and ask for a list of suppliers and contacts. You'll be surprised at the response you get. Some will push back, but most will be cordial and provide you with names and contact information. Of all of the ways to develop leads, this approach is one that salespeople are least likely to use, and yet it can generate huge opportunities because so few other salespeople use it! The supply chain is far more interwoven than most salespeople realize.

Who Are Your Customer's Customers?

Too many salespeople fail to dig in and understand who the customer is selling to. It's amazing what you'll find when you set out on a quest to gain new insights. Not only will you find out how to serve your existing customers better, but you also will hear insights regarding other people or companies you can contact.

A salesperson with whom I shared this idea said she had tried it, and when word got back to the customer, that company's marketing department contacted her. The marketing department was eager to learn what she found out from contacting their customers. The result from the effort was the salesperson picked up new leads and prospects that turned into clients, plus she became a hero and near cult-like figure with her original customer. From that point on, the salesperson virtually owned the customer, because they saw her as being so valuable.

Search Your Search

Your level of research needs to be only enough to provide you with what you need to make the first contact. There is zero reason to precede every call with the type of research you might have done for a college paper. Leveraging search engines such as Google can provide incredible insights, but the important thing to remember is there is no need to get carried away. I see far too many salespeople hesitate making a prospecting call because they want to do more online research. I use the Internet to do three things with regard to prospecting:

- ▶ Identify potential companies and people to prospect
- ▶ Identify specific contact information
- ▶ Identify a reason for the call

I can't emphasize enough the importance of not getting lost in the details. All you really need is one piece of information—that's it! The only exception to this would be if you're directly calling the CEO of a Fortune 500 company or are selling something so massive (such as jet aircraft or an entire office park complex) that you need to do significant research. Excuse me for assuming, but that's likely not you! Do a quick search, make the call, and move on.

If you insist on going deeper in using the Internet, I suggest you learn from who I believe is the smartest person on the subject: Sam Richter. He's amazing, and if you sit and watch how he leverages the search capabilities of Google, it will blow your mind. Check him out at www. SamRichter.com.

Calling Your Friends Is *Not* Prospecting

I'm not saying you can't talk with friends or associates. I'm simply suggesting that you talk to these people after you've done your prospecting. Here's a simple rule to keep in mind: unless someone has given you a solid referral in the last twelve to eighteen months, don't go thinking they're suddenly going to do it now if you spend more time with them.

Prospecting is about reaching out to people who have the potential to do business with you or can refer you to people who can. Everything else is not prospecting. Take a look at your calendar. Make a list of the phone calls you make. How much time are you spending each week talking with people who aren't helping you achieve your sales prospecting goals? When I ask salespeople this question, I always get a response that implies this is certainly not a problem for them. What is interesting is when I start probing and challenging them on their time, it's amazing how they begin to realize they *do* spend an enormous amount of time with people who are anything but sales prospects. Keep a log of all of the time you spend either meeting in person, making phone calls, or trading emails with people who are non-prospects. You'll be surprised at what you find after a week. Your objective should be to reduce that time by 50 percent—after all, it's impossible to eliminate all conversations of this type.

Use the time you save by turning it into additional sales prospecting time. If you were to add one hour a week to the amount of time you could be prospecting, it would equal an additional week in one year. There is zero reason for any salesperson—regardless of what they sell, how they sell it, or where they sell it—to be unable to develop a list of leads to keep them busy. If you're not finding enough leads, the first thing you should do is check your attitude. Chances are you're racing right past some great opportunities.

CHAPTER **8**

Are They Prospects or Merely Suspects?

N ot all prospects are prospects. In fact, I will argue that you and everyone else have a percentage of prospects or leads that aren't going anywhere. For one reason or another, you haven't come to grips yet with this reality.

Are You Gaming the System?

Thinking you can trick the system to succeed will ultimately catch up with you. Let me tell you about Wylie, an account manager I used to work with and his approach.

> Our sales manager, Bob, required each of us to meet with him weekly to review business and, in particular, how we were doing against our quarterly goal. Some quarters the meetings would go smoothly, because we were all having a good quarter. Other times it was ugly. During the bad quarters, we would dread sitting in the conference room waiting to be called into Bob's office to be jumped on and forced to listen to a litany of phrases to describe our incompetence.
>
> One quarter in particular was far more painful than any other. Business had gone soft, and with each passing week, the tongue lashings became louder and more intense. Well, that was the case

for everyone but Wylie. He would come out of the meeting and walk back into the conference room with a big grin. In fact, he would come back into the conference room as if nothing had happened, and then point to who Bob wanted to meet with next. It took us only a couple of weeks of seeing Wylie walk back from his meeting not feeling any pain before we asked what the deal was. Wylie was hesitant to respond, but then he confessed he wasn't giving Bob his real number. He stated he packed his pipeline with a lot of business that simply wasn't going to happen, but he didn't want to remove it.

One of the other salespeople challenged him on the logic, and his answer was amazing. He said how he knew the business wasn't going to occur, but if he took it out of the pipeline, Bob would chew him out week after week. His logic was to wait until week twelve of the quarter to take it out, and that way he would only get chewed out once. From his perspective, the way to avoid Bob chewing him out each week was to keep the pipeline full of bogus numbers.

I hope you're not like Wylie, although I do admit the guy was clever. I can't tell you the number of other salespeople with whom I've shared that story who have said they too have done something similar to game the system as a way of avoiding pain of one type or another.

What's in your pipeline? Are you stuffing it with leads or prospects that have little-to-zero chance of ever becoming customers? Are you holding on to them as a way to keep yourself from getting discouraged? Are you keeping them to make yourself look better than your peers? It's time to get real and treat your pipeline as sacred. You don't have time to play games with it, and you don't have time to use it as an ego builder. Your pipeline is your key to success. It's your key to making your number, so treat it as such!

I know I'm being blunt, but I'm tired of salespeople complaining they can't prospect. Let me share one more situation that, unfortunately, is going to hit home for many of you—especially those of you who are in a B2C business. When I was meeting with a team of salespeople recently to discuss prospecting, the topic of "bad prospects" came up. Every salesperson mentioned how they were guilty of having prospects who had little chance of ever becoming customers.

I asked, "If they have little chance of becoming a prospect, then why should we even think they're a prospect?" I love asking salespeople this question. The answers from the group varied, but the general overall answer was they were keeping them around because they were easy to talk to and they didn't have any better prospects to chase after. Think about that for a moment and the impact of what it means. To me it says salespeople are happy to go through the motions of spending time with bad prospects and not expecting results, all because they're too lazy or too ill-equipped to get real prospects. No wonder so many salespeople struggle to make their numbers! If you don't have good *prospects*, how do you expect to have good *customers*? If you don't have good customers, how do you expect to make your quota? It's not going to happen!

The answer is to focus your time to allow you to move prospects through the process faster, so you can determine if they truly are prospects or merely suspects. In the end, your goal should be to spend more time with fewer prospects, particularly prospects who have the best probability of becoming customers. Take a look at your CRM (Customer Relationship Management software). How many "prospects" do you have in your system who are anything but legitimate? Keeping those names in your system to give your boss the impression you're doing your job is not going to put food on the table!

I have a feeling there are those reading this book who suddenly want to put it down, pull up their pipelines, and determine what names they know they need to move out of their pipelines. If this is you, go ahead and do it now. I'll wait. When you finally realize you need to wipe out some of the stuff in your pipeline, remember one key thing: you're not removing the names from your CRM system or whatever tools you and your company use. What you're doing is taking them out of your active pipeline. The names and information are still valuable, but just not now.

You might have a marketing list, an email list, or whatever, and that's where the information should go. The lead that isn't going anywhere today may very well wind up being next year's hot new mega account. At the end of the day, it's important to realize how success as a salesperson is far more likely when you're allocating your time effectively and spending as much time as possible with those people most likely to buy *now*. I would much rather spend the day with three hot prospects than thirty leads that are going nowhere.

You've Got Suspects, Not Prospects

Too many prospects are nothing more than suspects pretending to be prospects. Prospects who are suspects don't walk around with a big sign around their neck saying, "Don't talk to me. I'm only a suspect!" No, they hide who and what they are for any number of reasons. Many times a suspect will engage with you repeatedly for no other reason than to gain information they can use elsewhere. Other suspects will engage because their bosses told them to meet with you. And still others will meet with you only because they don't have the courage to say "no" to your requests for a meeting. The absolute worst suspect is the one who engages with the salesperson just long enough to warrant a couple of free meals or box seats to a game or some other form of entertainment.

How many times have you spent too much time with what you thought was a great prospect, only to have them wind up being a suspect? If you can't tell the difference, there is no way you will ever achieve any level of success in sales. The sooner you can validate the intentions of the person with whom you are talking, the sooner you'll be using your time efficiently. Never forget the most valuable asset you have is your time, and the more time you spend with suspects, the less time you'll be able to spend with prospects.

Six Ways to Separate Prospects from Suspects

Here are some quick tips for determining who's a prospect and who's not.

1. Have they told you when they are going to make a decision?

Nothing is a bigger waste than spending your valuable time dealing with someone who only winds up saying they're not going to make a decision for months, or even years. Just because they're not going to make a decision for another year doesn't mean you ditch them. They will remain a good lead for you, but because it's a year away, the person isn't someone you need to spend time with now.

2. Have they shared with you a piece of proprietary information?

Proprietary information is something you would not be able to find any other way unless the person with whom you are talking shares it with you. The information might be personal or related to their business. I like this as a clue for one reason. A person is not going to share proprietary information with you unless they have confidence in you and feel there is a reason to do so. To put it another way, a person who has no intention of buying from you is most likely not going to share something that is proprietary in nature.

3. Do they have a need you can help them with?

If they're not willing to share a need with which you can help them, then stop wasting your time. There are far more important people to whom you can devote your time and effort. Don't get carried away with putting words into the customer's mouth as to how you could help them. A test I use: unless the customer says it with his or her own mouth, then don't believe it. Think about this for a moment. Would a person talk about a need if it weren't real? No. Let them tell you. Don't go putting words in their mouth.

4. Are you sure they're the decision maker?

Your ability to close a sale is going to go down dramatically if you're dealing with someone who is only conveying information to the real decision maker. A question I like to ask is, "How have you made decisions like this in the past?" A question like that is not threatening and will allow the prospect to share. Of course, what you're listening for are clues as to whether they will be making the decision. I also don't hesitate to ask, "Is there anyone else who will be involved in making the decision?" Again, it's straightforward and designed to ensure you're using your time in an effective manner.

5. Do they have the financial ability to buy?

At one time or another, we all have wasted the time of a salesperson by talking about something we *wanted* to buy, but had zero ability to actually buy.

What makes this so bad is many times the person wants to buy, but lacks the ability. So, the whole time they come across as being sincere in their intent to buy. A question I like to ask to gain the information is, "When you're making big decisions like this, what criteria do you consider?"

This is extremely difficult for the salesperson, because many times the customer still will blow smoke in your face claiming a low price is essential. I'm not concerned at this point if they do this, because I'll be fine if I do my job right and demonstrate value and total cost of ownership. What *does* concern me are signals that from a financial standpoint, they simply don't have the cash flow or credit to make the purchase.

6. **Has one of your competitors already clearly developed the customer's expectations?**

This could be a request for proposal (RFP) or bid quote to which you've been asked to respond. Very simple rule: If you didn't help write the RFP/bid, what makes you think you have a chance at winning it? If you didn't help write it, your competition probably did. If you're being invited to the party at this late stage, the only thing you're doing is providing the customer with information they can use to wrestle better terms from the salesperson who did help write the RFP. Sorry, but being invited late to the party is a kiss of death. The only thing you'll do is crank out a lot responses, and in the end you'll have nothing to show for it.

I do have one final item that I don't include as essential, but nonetheless it does help validate if the person with whom you're dealing is serious. Ask the person if they would do something for you after you end the conversation. For example, you could ask them if they would review and comment on information you'll send them soon. The reason this is a good gauge is because someone who is not interested in you at all will definitely *not* take the time to do anything "extra" you ask. Not only does it allow you to measure their interest, but it also helps you stay in their mind after the call.

The reason it's so important to validate your potential prospects is because you want to avoid wasting the most valuable asset you have—your time. Trust me, you do not want to spend a lot of time with people who have no intention of buying. Sure, there are times when you won't get answers to the previous questions and the lead still winds up being an awesome prospect and maybe even eventually a great customer. And yes, there are times when you *do* get answers to the above and the lead looks solid, but doesn't materialize at all. However, I have found when you do have answers to these questions and they line up with your expectations, ninety percent of the time you'll be well on your way to having a "developing customer." The questions more often than not work in helping you weed out the suspects so that you can focus on the prospects!

Price Does Not Belong in Prospecting

This issue is a sore spot to me, and although I've written about it in other chapters, I believe it's so important that it's worth writing about in this chapter, too. Everyone wants to believe they're going after only high-value prospects. However, far too often the strategy they're using is attracting low-value prospects. If anything in your sales prospecting strategy is price-oriented, then guess what? You're naturally going to attract low-value prospects.

You might think that's fine if business is so slow that low-value prospects are better than no prospects. But know that we will naturally attract what we set out to attract. If you talk price, you'll get price; if you talk benefits, you'll get benefits. The key is to focus everything you do on helping the customer with their needs and allowing them to build confidence in you and what you provide. Let me get even more blunt: low price is not a prospecting tool. If you are forced to use price to attract prospects, then you haven't figured out how to distinguish yourself from the competition. Differentiating yourself through benefits leads to high-value prospects.

A key reason I'm against using price as a prospecting tool is because once you start using it, you and your customers will become addicted to it. The level of profit you lose will be huge, both in the short term and the long term. Sadly, you will become slightly blind to this, because focusing on low price will be your go-to method.

To help keep your focus on the needs of the prospect, make sure you're asking them questions that get them to expand upon their problem. Remember, your objective is to either help them overcome a problem or allow them to achieve a gain. That's it. Don't overcomplicate things. Keep your focus on the customer's wants and needs and you'll avoid having to go down the price trap road.

When you focus your prospecting approach in this manner, you'll find yourself quickly building up a library of great questions you can ask. You'll become extremely comfortable and confident in asking such questions. The end result? You'll find yourself dealing with even higher-value customers than before, all while moving further away from price as a prospecting tool.

CHAPTER 9

Best Practices for Making the Initial Contact

Whether it is a name your marketing department gave you or a name you identified as a potential lead, there comes a time for you to make initial contact. The old expression we've all heard is true: initial impressions make a lasting impression. I don't say this to scare anyone away from making a call or sending an email—in sales, until you make contact nothing happens. What I'm saying is you do need to make sure your initial contact contains something that will benefit the other person.

Your Prospects Don't Care about You

Too many salespeople make the mistake of thinking the initial call must be about themselves or their company. Unless you're somebody famous or you have a product everyone has to have, I hate to break the news to you, but your prospect couldn't care less. What does this mean to you? It means you need to quit making stupid phone calls, sending out lousy emails, or even leaving poor voicemails that extoll who you are and how great your company is. Your prospects simply don't care!

An example I like to use is how movies display the credits. When you see a movie, you don't have to sit through five minutes of scrolling credits before the movie begins. It's not until the end of the movie where we see the credits. The director knows he or she needs to pull you into the movie quickly, or you'll give up on it. Save your data dump, because starting off with it will only ensure the prospect will dump you.

Your prospect didn't wake up this morning drooling over the possibility you might call them today. They have their own problems. To the prospect, you're no different and certainly no better than any other salesperson who is thinking the same way. Just because you took the time to write what you think is a great email or leave a perfect voicemail doesn't mean the other person is going to suddenly view it as the breakthrough insight for which they've been waiting. Regardless of what you sell, you have more competitors than ever. Each one is ready to jump in and grab the business you're trying to get. Avoid self-serving blather about how many years you've been in business and the awards you've won! Once again, the prospect does not care.

Too many salespeople start off the first email or phone call wasting everyone's time by introducing themselves and their company. This means you can permanently delete the "capabilities presentation" the marketing department built for you five years ago. I'm not saying you don't introduce yourself, but if it's more than a few words, don't be surprised if the other person blows you off. Cut to the chase and get to the point of *why* the two of you need to connect quickly! Save all of your "look at me and how wonderful my company is" information for your high school reunion.

Your Goal Is a First Date

At the most basic level, you want to make contact with a lead, preferably with a phone call, and do two things:

1. Find out one piece of information about the company and/or person with whom you're talking.
2. Secure a next step: either an in-person meeting or another phone call at a designated time.

The first call is not the time to overcomplicate things. Too many salespeople make the mistake of trying to do a huge information dump on the first call, and it winds up going nowhere. (If what you're selling is a quick sale with a short sales cycle, then you certainly should be speeding the process along, but it still does not give you the right to do a full data dump on the prospect.) Your first call should create a level of confidence and gain leverage to have a second call.

During your second call, dig deeper and truly qualify the prospect to ensure they're really a prospect and not a suspect. Use the criteria outlined in the preceding chapter. Attempting to complete all of that on the first call is rarely doable, and too many times if you try to do it all, the end result will be nothing.

Three Ways to Get the First Date

Your goal is to capture the other person's attention quickly and help them see enough value in you that they will share with you information you can use on the next call. Here are the three best-practice approaches I have seen deliver the best results for both B2B and B2C:

- ► Referral/connection
- ► Key insight/information
- ► Value statement

Below are brief examples of how to use each one; however, in later chapters, I will share in more detail how to use each one.

Referral/Connection

This is the easiest to use. Put simply, you are using a person's name or the name of a company in which the person you're contacting will see value.

TELEPHONE EXAMPLE

"Hello, Ross, I'm Mark Hunter with Apex Systems. Pacific Mountain Company found a huge amount of savings through a program I helped them with. Would you have time next week for me to come by so I can show you?"

The key is being prepared to respond, regardless of how the other person replies to your question. If they say, "No, I don't have time," your response would be either "When would be a good time to meet?" or "How are you doing in cutting costs in today's climate?" Your objective with the follow-up question is to impart knowledge you can use when you connect with them at a later time.

EMAIL EXAMPLE

> **Subject:** Pacific Mountain
>
> Audrey,
>
> Pacific Mountain was able to reduce their costs significantly using a program we helped them install. In the first year, they reduced spending by 15%.
>
> Knowing the pressure to grow earnings, I thought you would be interested in knowing more. I'm Mark Hunter with Apex Systems. Please feel free to email or call and we can set up a time to discuss.
>
> Thanks,
> Mark Hunter
> Apex Systems
> 555-555-5555

Notice how it is direct and short. No one has time to read long emails. Your objective with the email isn't to provide them so much information that they can readily make a decision, but rather to help them realize they need to contact you.

Key Insight/Information

This approach works great in industries where change is frequent, such as evolving technology, government regulation, or new competitors entering the field. Your objective is to merely convey to them you have some critical insights they will find of interest.

"Hello Reuben, this is Mark Hunter, with Hunter Financial, and I have the new IRS regulations that have just come out regarding pensions and how they affect people like you. Call me at 555-555-5555 and we can set up a time to discuss, again Mark Hunter, 555-555-5555."

Value Statement

This process is tied to making a power statement about something, and then asking for the person's input or for a meeting to discuss it more. Of the three best-practice approaches, salespeople use this one the most. For this reason, I steer clients away from using it so they can differentiate themselves from every other salesperson.

Sheila, I'm Mark Hunter with Apex Systems. There is a real push by companies to grow their sales by automating the back office. How is your company approaching the back office and its effectiveness?"

With this approach, the key is to engage the other person quickly in a conversation and then use what they share as the basis for your next question. Your objective with this approach is the same as with the others—to gain a key piece of information you can use as the foundation for your next conversation.

These three approaches work regardless if you're using the telephone, email, voicemail, social media, or even text. The more you use these techniques, the more comfortable you will become with them, and you will begin to understand better which ones (or variations of them) work best for you. As you read the rest of the book, you'll uncover more ways to use these three approaches.

The Art of the Second Date

Do not think for a moment these three techniques are always going to work the first time you reach someone. Many times it will take a second, third, fourth, and subsequent contacts before you get any sort of information that equips you to move forward. This is why it's important for you to have multiple approaches. Think of how your prospect is receiving your messages. If you were a prospect and a salesperson reaching out to you used the same message and approach repeatedly, you'd become annoyed with them. The best prospector is the one who uses multiple approaches and is comfortable moving back and forth between them as situations dictate. In the chapters that follow, we will break down the mechanics step by step to show you in even more depth how to use these approaches.

However, one item I can't emphasize enough is the need to keep a record of what you're using. This includes the message, the time you sent it, and the delivery method. This is why a good CRM system such as Salesforce can earn its keep. If you think you can use one delivery method for your entire prospecting strategy, think again. What you like may not be what your prospect likes.

The one activity that causes more sales prospecting programs to fail than any other is the lack of follow-up and willingness to keep contacting the other person. I have talked about it in earlier chapters, and I will continue to talk about it. You must be willing to keep following up. When you use the techniques laid out in this book and combine them with persistent follow-up, your probability for success will increase significantly.

10

Does the Telephone Still Work?

"**M**r. Watson, come here. I want to see you." Those last five words are still as relevant today as they were when Alexander Graham Bell, the inventor of the telephone, first said them to Thomas Watson on March 10, 1876. Bell wasn't making a sales call. (Or maybe he was? I'll let you answer that.) Those five words—"I want to see you"—are the key reason I believe the telephone is still an excellent prospecting tool. Sadly, there are plenty of salespeople who fail to realize the telephone is an effective way to prospect. It doesn't matter how much anyone says otherwise, I'm a firm believer the telephone is an amazing prospecting tool when used right and with the right expectations.

When I was speaking at an industry association meeting, I asked the audience of more than 200 salespeople who worked in both B2B and B2C why they didn't like using the telephone for prospecting. Their answers came down to three main reasons:

- ▶ Cold calling doesn't work.
- ▶ I can't reach anybody and nobody answers.
- ▶ I'm not comfortable on the phone.

The telephone will deliver results when used properly. I'm not going to say it will deliver as fruitful results as it did ten years ago, but then again, that is also true about a number of other things. Being successful in prospecting today requires you to use multiple communication tools. The more tools you use well, the better you'll be at not just prospecting, but also the entire sales process.

Cold Calling vs. Informed Calling

There is no reason with all of the information available today for anyone to have to make a cold call. The return on investment making cold calls is simply no longer there for most industries, and the speed with which governments are adding laws regulating cold calling is only adding to its rapid demise. I do not long for a return to the days of having the home telephone ringing nonstop every evening, only to hear a "robocall" or someone reading from a script, informing me of some *amazing* offer available only if I take action now. Automated dialing systems combined with sophisticated software keep cold calling alive, and even with those advancements, I would say its prognosis is terminal.

The biggest reason I believe cold calling is dead is because it takes too much time, and the most valuable sales resource is your time. Informed calling is a better approach, and it's *informed* because the call you're making has a reason. The reason I want to call you is to gain information, because I know I can be of assistance to you based on something I've already learned about you. My information might be limited to knowing you're in the same industry as other clients with whom I work, but for some specific reason, I feel we should talk. When you're making "informed calls," you're providing a service to the person you're calling.

And remember, don't let yourself believe you make one call and that's it. I'll give you a personal example. Years ago, I was not a coffee drinker. My wife was constantly trying to sell me on the merits of coffee and why I would like it, but I resisted for years. She offered to make me coffee on hundreds of occasions—weekly, at a minimum, and frequently multiple times the same day. Finally I gave in, tried it, and soon thereafter began to view coffee as one of my major "food groups." Today, I couldn't think of not having coffee! If my wife had asked once and then never again, I might never have become the coffee drinker I am today. My wife knew I would see value in it and persisted. The same thing applies to your prospecting approach. Don't think for a moment a single call is all that's needed.

You Can't Hide—I'll Find You

Salespeople also are quick to say phone numbers are hard to get. Yes, they can be hard to get, but that means they're also hard for your competition to get. There are plenty of ways to uncover phone numbers, and it all starts with saying, "I'm not going to let an obstacle stand in my way."

TEN WAYS TO GET A PHONE NUMBER

1. Check the company's website.
2. Do a profile search on LinkedIn for anyone working at that company or check the company's profile page.
3. Do a profile search on LinkedIn for someone who used to work at the company you're trying to reach, and ask them for a phone number.
4. Call the Chamber of Commerce or a similar organization in the city where the company is located.
5. Contact a supplier of the company you're trying to reach.
6. Use Twitter to find the company's handle and any contact info.
7. Check Facebook to find a company's business page.
8. Contact an industry trade association.
9. Use www.data.com, a great tool provided by Salesforce that contains information for millions of people.
10. Search your own company's CRM system and files.

Yes, some of the ten ways are a bit out there, but that's why I listed them. Anyone who says they can't find a phone number is simply not trying. The reason they're saying they can't get a phone number is because to them, it's the easiest excuse as to why they won't use the telephone for prospecting.

An added bonus that can come out of searching for a phone number is gaining a valuable piece of information you can use in your first call. This is why I say there's no reason to ever have to make a true cold call. It's an "informed call," because you either have a specific piece of information about them you want to ask or you have another insight you want to share.

They're Not Answering. Now What?

Yes, I know people don't answer the phone. Hey, I'm guilty of not answering it, too. Why don't people answer the phone? They don't want to get stuck on the phone with a salesperson! Yes, I just said it! People will, however, use voicemail messages as a screening tool. Leave a good voicemail and you earn points; leave a bad message and you'll be banished to the pool of permanent rejection. (I've devoted chapter 14 exclusively to the art and science of voicemail.)

If you believe calling a prospect is rude, then let me ask you another question. Do you believe you offer your customers something beneficial? Of course you do! That's why you do what you do! With that said, never allow yourself to believe every call you make is going to reach the other person at a perfect time. You will be rejected and ignored, but that is simply why you get paid what you do. If prospecting were easy, your company wouldn't need you and/or they wouldn't need to be paying you as much as they do. The game is persistence. You must be persistent, because tenacity will ultimately win. You may not reach the prospect today, tomorrow, or even next week. It may take months or even a year, but you will succeed.

In my years of working with salespeople, I have found the key reason they're not comfortable on the phone is because they're not willing to be persistent enough. They become overwhelmed by the rejection and the silence from the people they're trying to prospect. As their mind plays games from the rejection, they begin to doubt the techniques they're using. Left unchecked, this doubt becomes a downward spiral, leading to a complete lack of success and significant disappointment. The chapters to follow spell out step by step the mechanics of prospecting using various communication tools. The methods work if you allow them to. Successful prospecting is the goal, and there's no reason to doubt your ability to succeed.

CHAPTER 11

Customer Engagement Dos and Don'ts

Salespeople frequently ask me, "When is the right time to make the call?" My response is, "Right now!" If you don't make the call now, when will you make it? Will you ever make it? If there is any chance you won't make the call another time, then make it *now*— regardless of what you know or don't know. I have had people claim what I'm about to say is not right, but I believe I'm right at least nine times out of ten. Yes, it sounds strange and flies in the face of conventional wisdom, but I truly believe *a bad call is still better than no call.* Believe me when I say I've had some contentious discussions with sales managers and salespeople about this, but I stick with it. Momentum has a way of creating momentum. The first call one morning might be bad and the second one might still be bad, but eventually things will begin to kick in and the calls will start going the way you want them to go.

Earlier in this book, I talked about scheduling time to prospect, and a key part of that is blocking time that will have you on the phone when you're most likely to reach your prospect. For a lot of industries, Monday mornings can be a bad time to make prospecting calls, but this is not true of all industries. If you work for a temporary staffing firm, Monday mornings can be an ideal time to make prospecting calls, because that's when your prospects are suddenly realizing they're short-staffed for the week. The same is true of Fridays for some industries, especially Friday afternoons. Salespeople who tell me this is a bad time to call are the same ones who in my mind are just looking for a reason to start the weekend early. For people selling to the construction industry, Friday afternoons can be a perfect time to call prospects, because often they're winding things up for the week, are more laid back, and are more willing to talk. Never rule out a day or time of day just because you think it won't work for your industry.

What's most important is that you are willing to try. You don't know what you don't know, and many times a false assumption can wind up hurting your prospecting efforts—and ultimately your bottom line—more than you realize. I also have found huge variances depending on the time of year. Just because you're not making much progress calling on Fridays in September doesn't mean Fridays won't be the perfect day of week to call in February. New salespeople who try calling at different times often have more success with the prospects that veterans can't seem to crack. The new salespeople are successful because they're willing to try what others feel will not work.

Pour the Coffee and Make the Call

I can't stress enough the importance of early morning phone calls! There's nothing like starting your day off and running by making a couple of key calls at the beginning of the day. Even if the calls are to friendly customers with whom you work on a regular basis, it's a great way to boost your positive attitude and get you going. Once you've made one or two calls to current customers to warm yourself up, keep the momentum going by making as many prospecting calls as you can in the time you've allotted for prospecting. Reaching out to people early in the morning before things get going conveys to the other person you're a hard-charging person they can count on. Yes, there are some who won't respond positively to the phone call before eight in the morning, but they're in the minority.

One of the best benefits of making early morning phone calls is you are far more likely to actually make them. Saying you're going to make them later in the day is setting yourself up to not make them at all. The reason is simple. As your day progresses, other things will get in your way, and before you know it the day is gone and the prospecting phone calls remain nothing more than an idea. This is one more reason it is so important to dedicate times in your calendar to prospect and not allow distractions to get in the way.

Use the time before eight in the morning as the perfect window to reach the person you've been unable to reach at other times of the day. A strategy that works well is to make your first two attempts at reaching someone during the normal part of the day. Make the third attempt before eight, and I know you'll be amazed at who you are able to reach. Calling before eight most likely will provide you with the highest number of phone calls that do not get tied up by the gatekeeper. Either you'll reach the person you're looking for, or you'll be able to leave a voicemail.

I am such a strong believer in early morning prospecting calls that whenever I'm working with a salesperson who is struggling with prospecting, the first thing I ask is how many phone calls they are making each day before eight. The response is typically something like, "I don't make early morning phone calls because nobody is in and I'm still getting my day organized." To me that is code for "I'm lazy." Early morning calls work, because even if the person doesn't answer, you still have a great opportunity to leave a voicemail message.

How early is too early? The answer will vary by industry and even by geography. My rule is anytime after seven thirty is fair game to make calls, but for many industries (such as the building trades and warehousing) you can call as early as six thirty.

"Five after Five"

A Houston-based client with whom I've had the privilege to work for years provided me with an outstanding way to remember making calls at the end of the day. Kathryn is as aggressive a sales leader as you will ever meet. When she shared with me "five after five," a strategy that had helped her immensely at the start of her sales career, I knew it was awesome. The idea is simple! Make five more prospecting calls after 5:00 p.m.

Over the years I've taken her idea and shared it with other people, who have then run with it even further by making it their mission to do "eight before eight." That's right! Eight phone calls before 8 a.m. I love it! This idea reflects what my good friend and sales leader Jeb Blount loves to say: "One more call. You always have time to make one more call!"

Who Takes Holidays?

Time and time again, I have found making prospecting calls during holiday weeks will pay off well. I'm always surprised at how people behave differently knowing there's a holiday coming; the same is true of many of the prospects you're trying to reach. Calling during a holiday week may result in actually speaking with the person you've been trying to reach, but who rarely answers the phone in normal prospecting times. Your contact is more likely to answer the phone during a holiday week because his or her administrative assistant (or whoever typically handles incoming calls) may be taking vacation that week.

Salespeople in most industries are quick to say that when December rolls around, nobody wants to see or talk with them, so it just doesn't make sense to prospect. This attitude, along with the idea that the new year is coming soon, makes salespeople think they should wait until January and start fresh. I can't argue more *against* this shortsighted thinking. Thinking you can't prospect in December is accepting the fact one month out of twelve (or eight percent of your year) is not effective. Would your boss find it acceptable if you said you were taking eight percent of the year off? No, but that is exactly what too many salespeople do.

Never allow yourself to think getting new customers is not a good idea beginning in mid-November and through the end of the year. People and companies have money to spend this time of year, often budgeted money they need to spend *before* the end of the year. You never will know who has money unless you make the call and find out! Sales cycles during December never follow the norm. For the customer looking to spend money before it's lost, the buying cycle is shortened. For others who can't buy until the new year, it might be lengthened. The key is to not allow your traditional sales thinking to cloud your willingness to connect with a prospect.

When you stop prospecting in December, you also are telling yourself you don't expect to do much business in January. You'll need January to make prospecting calls just to get appointments set up. The best way you can help yourself in making your first-quarter number is by using December to prospect, so you will have a full calendar of customer appointments in January.

A Dallas-based company I was working with suffered from a January slump. Each year their sales in January were always low, and what did come in never came in until the end of the month. After talking with the management team, it became clear why. The sales force believed nobody wanted to talk with them in December, so they spent the month doing zero prospecting. I challenged their thinking, and with a lot of prodding, I had the sales force begin calling aggressively throughout the entire month. When I say "the entire month," I really mean the entire month, including that week between Christmas and New Year's Day when many people are on vacation. Note, however: calling when many people are on vacation is the only time I'm not a proponent of leaving a voicemail. The last thing most people want when they come back to work is to face a voicemail inbox full of messages from salespeople.

Sure, the number of prospects the team was able to reach was lower due to the holidays, but the people with whom the sales team did speak were absolutely amazing. Leads and prospects they did reach on the telephone were in a more laid-back mood and willing to talk about their business. They were shocked a salesperson would even be working! The end result was the prospects viewed the salespeople in a favorable light and were far more likely to agree to a meeting. In the end, the pushback I took from the sales team turned to gratitude because they started the year with sales appointments on the calendar. These meetings, in turn, resulted in an increase in business, making January unlike any of their previous Januarys.

The example I shared may have been based on the last two weeks of December, but the same results can be expected during the week of Thanksgiving and other holiday weeks. To me, using these weeks to your advantage is the easiest way to vault ahead of your competitor. If you sell in an industry where continuous ordering by customers is the norm, being aggressive during these weeks is the easiest way to show that you're different from the competition. It's why I say if you're in this type of business, you want to be aggressive in calling all of your competitor's customers. You want to be the vendor the customer calls for the last-minute emergency order their normal vendor can't fill. This is like printing money! When I get to help someone fill an urgent order, I look like a hero. People don't forget a hero. You help them once, and then you help them again, and before long you're their primary supplier, having taken the customer away from your competition. Your ability to demonstrate service during holiday weeks can do more for building your business than nearly anything else.

CHAPTER 12

Prospecting Tools—The Telephone

I love listening to salespeople make prospecting calls. I'm sure the majority of the people to whom I am listening would say otherwise, but it's all part of learning how to become a better prospector. With one particular sales team, I was coaching a talented woman making B2B and B2C calls. She had a great personality and knew what she needed to do, but one thing was standing in her way. She could not get over the hurdle that a phone call could go in a direction other than what she had planned. She knew enough about the prospect to make the call worthwhile, but her entire focus was on the conversation she was *planning* to have with the decision maker. Whenever the call went into voicemail, she became flustered. If somebody other than the decision maker took the call, she would freeze up and not know what to do next.

Her sales results were far less than they should have been, especially for someone who was as smart as she was. In coaching her, I found the only way she could be successful was by having a script for each scenario in which she might find herself. Assembling all the scripts she needed took time, and initially she was hesitant to do it. It paid off in the end. Within a few weeks of using the scripts, she became comfortable enough to not need them, and within 90 days she was getting the results she should have had all along. I share this story not to say I'm always an advocate of using a script. I generally don't like scripts, as they limit your ability to truly listen, but I do like them as a training tool to help gain confidence and momentum.

As you work through these chapters, don't downplay the role a script can play. In future chapters, I will provide you with sample scripts, and I encourage you to use them to guide you in developing ones that will work for you. Your goal is to become proficient and confident enough to not use any scripts; however, I believe you will always want to maintain a list of key talking points for specific situations. I recommend such a list for even the most veteran salespeople. Having your talking points written down will keep you from slowly drifting, as I have seen many salespeople do over time. They start off focused, but within a few weeks or months, they start taking shortcuts that ultimately lead to a decrease in their effectiveness. The first rule is to make sure you use each call as an opportunity to learn something you can use on your next call. If you make calls to different types of prospects or industries, I strongly suggest you cluster the similar ones together. Devote one calling period to a single industry or customer type. Doing so will allow you to take what you learn from one call and apply it to the next. Many sales teams I work with have embraced this concept, and later they come back to me and say how effective it is. As a result, the salespeople learn more and learn faster, and they come across on the phone much more in tune with the prospect's industry.

The second rule is to never ask if it is a good time to talk. I despise this question for one simple reason: the person you're calling wasn't expecting your call and they weren't sitting around with nothing to do. If somebody asks me if it's a good time to talk, my response is a fast, "No," followed by a click of the phone. There are salespeople who come back to me and say it's rude to not ask if it's a good time to talk. My argument is the prospect doesn't comprehend yet how much value I can bring to them, so why would I be so shortsighted as to give them an easy way out of the call? Remember, your objective is not to have a thirty-minute call. Your objective is a two- or three-minute phone call, or just long enough to gain an insight and to arrange for a second meeting.

The third rule is to make sure your voice has energy, is positive in tone, and can be heard clearly. I recommend salespeople make their prospecting phone calls standing up and with a quality headset. Standing up simply gives you more energy, which will come through in your voice.

A good headset frees up your hands, and it's amazing how much more energetic we are when we talk with our hands. You can be incredibly smart, have the best product or service, and know exactly what to say, but you may never get a chance with the prospect if your voice is timid, soft, and lacks confidence.

The final rule is to never make the purpose of your call something like "I'm just checking in" or "I thought I would see how you're doing." These might be perfect if you're calling a family member, but they are not appropriate for prospecting, regardless of whom you might be calling in any B2B situation and most B2C situations. Your objective with each call is to bring value. Remember, it's about them, not about you. In B2C there occasionally will be times when you could lead with this type of an opening, but only when you already have a good relationship with the person you're calling. The fallout I have seen happen far too often is the B2C salesperson begins to use this approach occasionally, and over time they become too relaxed and begin using it as their primary method to start calls.

Ten Best Practices for Prospecting with the Telephone

Follow these proven guidelines when prospecting by telephone.

1. **Make the call about the prospect, not about you.**

    The reason for the call must be to provide the prospect with information or insight they will find of value. Have three questions ready you can ask them and/or three benefit statements in which they will find value.

2. **Speak with energy and believe in yourself.**

    If you don't believe in yourself and speak with confidence and energy, why should you expect the prospect to pay attention?

3. **If a door closes on you, find a different door.**

    Don't think for a moment there's only one phone number you can call.

4. Be prepared, regardless of how the call is answered.

Calls can go one of three ways—your prospect answers, a gate-keeper answers, or it rolls to voicemail. Each one requires a different type of response from you. Be prepared no matter which way it goes.

5. Always use a quality headset to make your calls.

We are more effective in our communication when we speak with our hands, even when the other person can't see us.

6. Use the day wisely, and keep records of when you call and what is said.

Many prospects are best reached before eight in the morning or after five in the early evening. Experiment with different times to learn what types of prospects are most likely to respond at what time.

7. Never think one call is all it's going to take.

Be prepared to call the same prospect a number of times to finally be able to break through. A strategy I like is six contacts in a month. If after a month I'm not successful, I will then back off for sixty to ninety days and then repeat the process.

8. Never leave the same voicemail twice with the same person.

Leaving the same message repeatedly is a quick way for the person you are trying to reach to have zero respect for you. Also remember that you will increase your odds of reaching the person by calling different days and at different times.

9. Call right before the top of the hour to reach busy people.

Most meetings start at the top of the hour, which means the one time you might be able to catch the person is just before a meeting starts.

10. Never give up.

It's easy to think the telephone isn't effective and that using email or even social media is the better way to go. The only reason people think that is because they are not willing to put in the effort and time to make telephone prospecting a part of their overall prospecting plan.

CHAPTER **13**

Starting the Conversation

You develop your plan to guide you through whichever way the phone call might go, you call, and the person you're trying to reach answers. It is now game on! Go! The first words out of your mouth will set the tone for whether or not the call is going to go well. The key is to have a benefit statement or pertinent news update you can share with the prospect you're calling, built around one of the three strategies shared in chapter 9 (referral/connection, key insights/information, value statement). When you approach the call in this manner, it's not a cold call—it's an informed call.

I Wasn't Expecting That to Happen

Whenever you make a call, it can wind up going one of three ways. You must be ready for your call to go any of these directions:

- ▶ You reach the person you're trying to reach.
- ▶ A gatekeeper answers and blocks you from getting any further.
- ▶ You reach the voicemail of the person you're trying to reach.

The challenge is that each scenario requires a completely different response. If you're not prepared for whichever one might happen, you are more apt to damage your ability to ultimately make your sale. At one time or another, we've all made a phone call to someone fully expecting to get their voicemail, only to wind up having them actually answer. Who among us hasn't had this happen when someone is calling us? Our phone rings, we answer and the other person is shocked and confused as to what to do next. Can you relate? The number of stories I could share from my own experience are most likely not too different from yours. The key is having a plan for each situation that could happen when you make a call. In the chapters to follow, we will break down each one in detail.

Before we jump into how to handle the different ways a call can go, there are some universal rules that apply.

Never start a phone call asking a stupid question about the weather! I'm tired of listening to salespeople who call me asking me how the weather is. Using a question about the weather to start a conversation with somebody you don't know is silly. This is particularly important if you're selling in a B2B environment. There, you're dealing with people who value their time. It's hard to find a businessperson who does not have more on their plate than they have time to get done. Respect their time. When you call, give them something meaningful to consider.

Telephone Scripts You Need

On the following pages are a number of sample benefit statement/ question templates you can use to start the conversation. These are the same opening statement and question templates I've shared with thousands of salespeople. I've broken them down into five types to provide you with as much assistance as possible. *Do not* view any one of them as something you must strictly follow. These are only templates meant to guide you in developing what will work best for you and your situation.

The questions I ask the prospect are designed to uncover one need with which I can assist them, and to share enough information to allow the prospect to see I can help them. I do not believe in going beyond these initial goals, unless the prospect is freely engaging in further conversation. If that's the case, go for more by asking questions and allowing the prospect to control the conversation.

Your goal is to develop over time three unique benefit statements and/or three unique pertinent pieces of news that the type of person who you're trying to reach would find of interest. What you share must be of benefit to them, not you. And it must be information they can understand, regardless of whether they know exactly what you do.

Yes, this will require time, but I guarantee it will increase your results. Don't get hung up on having three different statements or pieces of information for each person. Typically, what works for one person works for another person in the same industry. This is why I'm a firm believer in trying to cluster prospecting calls by industry, as discussed in an earlier chapter.

Telephone scripts to start a call

B2B, short sales cycle, with goods or services that are purchased regularly:

1. Hello, I'm _____ with _____. Are you the person in charge of buying _____? How are doing dealing with _____? How interested would you be in _____?

2. Hello, is this _____? I'm _____ with _____. I believe you know [name of person]. They have been able to _____ by working with us. What would those types of results look like for you?

3. Hello, I'm _____ with _____. We have _____ that works with _____ which you're already using. Who is your current supplier? How are they doing for you? Can you tell me more?

B2B, long sales cycle, where typically there are multiple decision makers and the purchase is considered a major investment:

1. Hello _____. Thanks for taking my call. I'm _____ with _____. There are new studies out regarding _____. This looks like it will create significant _____ in less time than before. Where does something like this fit into your business plan?

(continued on next page)

(continued from previous page)

2. Hello _____. I'm _____ with _____. We have been working with _____ and have seen major _____, which from what I've been told is something you're working on, too. How is the project going for you?

3. Hello _____. I'm _____ with _____. I just saw where you announced _____. We just got done helping _____ do the same thing. What are the goals you're looking to achieve from this?

B2B, new product or service the prospect is not currently using and may not even be familiar with:

1. Hello, is this _____? My name is _____ with _____. What have been the results you've been able to see from _____? I've heard the same thing from others and that's why _____. What would your business look like if you were to _____?

2. Hello, I'm _____ with _____. We help others like you achieve _____. Have you been able to _____ in the last year? How do you intend to handle _____ going forward?

3. Hello, I'm _____ with _____. Your company has been able to achieve significant progress doing _____. What do you feel has been the reason for your success? We have some items that would allow you to _____, resulting in _____. How important would something like that be to you?

B2C, product or service is most likely already being used now but being bought from a competitor:

1. Hi, I'm _____ with _____. Do you currently use a _____ to help you with _____? What has been your experience with them?

2. Good evening, I'm _____ with _____. Are you familiar with _____? Are you aware _____ could help you minimize _____?

3. Hello, I'm _____ with _____. I believe you know _____. I was just talking with them, as they've been our customer for a long time. They said I might want to reach out to you. What has been your experience with _____?

B2C, longer sales cycle, where the purchase is viewed as major decision:

1. Hello, _____ I'm _____ with _____. New information has just come out regarding _____. Have you seen it yet? How do you feel this might impact your _____?

2. Hello, is this _____? My name is _____ with _____. A number of people like you have been calling me asking for assistance with _____, so I thought I would reach out and ask you how much of a concern _____ is to you.

3. Hello, is this _____? My name is _____ and I'm with _____. There is a new trend people are seeing real benefit in, allowing them to _____. Have you heard from friends or others about this?

All You Need is One

The goal with each sample script is to allow you to get a conversation going. You have two objectives: make the prospect feel comfortable with you, and gain one insight from them. With the insight you learn, you want to establish a time for the next appointment.

To help get you to your goal of gaining at least one piece of information you can use, you must be prepared to handle the response the prospect gives you. There are "sales experts" who believe it's important to control the call and not allow the prospect to gain the upper hand. I say a better approach is to listen to the prospect and go in the direction they want to go. If I am not a match for the prospect, then I would rather find out now—rather than move through the entire sales process only to be rejected at the close. Remember, the title of this book is *High-Profit Prospecting*, and it's all about finding prospects who will give you the greatest opportunity to close more sales at a higher price. My goal is to find prospects to whom I can bring value at full price.

Recently, I called a prospect with whom I felt I would be a good fit. To start the conversation, I found an update to a new piece of federal legislation that was going to impact their industry. I began the conversation asking if he had seen the new information, and when he said he had not, I was able to share one point from what I had read. From there I was able to ask a couple of questions on his thoughts, which in turn led to an interesting discussion. The prospect shared insights with me about his company, and at the same time told me how impressed he was that I was aware of the legislation, leading him to view me as someone who could bring value to his company. The call lasted less than five minutes, and I came away with insights I needed and an agreement to meet in thirty days.

The time I spent researching and reading information before the call was less than ten minutes. Combine that with the brief phone call, and in less than fifteen minutes total, I was able to go from at best having a lead to now having what was shaping up to be a valuable prospect. I ultimately closed the deal, and the prospect became a major customer for my company.

The best way to respect time is to use it to your advantage by sharing key information that allows the customer to understand you care about their business and can help them. I will always believe opening the conversation with something meaningful will lead to discovering more information from the prospect, and ultimately you'll end up with a conversation that benefits you both.

14

Does Anybody Listen to Voicemail?

L et's not kid ourselves—the vast majority of phone calls go to voice-mail. But that's not a good enough reason to avoid the telephone for prospecting. In fact, I think voicemail, when used properly, is perfect for prospecting.

An excuse I hear far too often is, "Why leave a message when nobody will return it anyway? They're most likely not even listening to it!" Excuse me for a moment, but I'm going to be blunt: the reason prospects aren't returning your messages is because you're leaving garbage messages. That's right! Garbage messages. Seriously, if you were a prospect and received one of your prospecting messages, would you return it? No! Would you even bother to listen to the entire message? I doubt it! We've answered the question as to why you're not getting callbacks—the reason is you. But voicemail messages can and do work when you know what you're doing.

What Did They Say?

How many times have you started listening to a voicemail message, only to realize a few seconds into it that the message is not worth your time? We all have. How many times have you listened to a pathetic voice-mail message and wound up listening to it just to see how ridiculous the person can be? I bet you have, and I know I have on more than one occasion. We have allowed ourselves to believe voicemail messages don't work because of the numerous bad messages we've had land in our voicemail boxes. We also have believed voicemail doesn't work because nobody returns a message. Just because others haven't been successful does not mean you won't be. Voicemail works when it's used properly and your expectations are reasonable. I treat voicemail like one tool in my prospecting toolbox. As is the case with each tool, it has unique advantages over other prospecting tools.

Pros of Voicemail

- ▶ Prospect can listen to your voice and feel your confidence and energy.
- ▶ You can leave a tight and concise message that demonstrates you respect the prospect's time.
- ▶ You have a chance to build awareness with the prospect. Your messages serve as a form of advertising, helping the prospect become more familiar with you.
- ▶ You can leave messages at different times of the day, which shows the prospect you're willing to work hard.
- ▶ The prospect can listen to messages at a time convenient for them.

Cons of Voicemail

- ▶ Learning how to leave a good message takes time and practice.
- ▶ Depending on your CRM system and the tools you have, the information you leave might be harder to get into the system.
- ▶ There is a risk of the prospect not listening to the message; however, this risk is no greater than with any other prospecting tool you might use.

Will these be the same pros and cons five years from now? I don't have an answer to that, but I'm not going to worry about it. My goal is to make this quarter's number, and I know voicemail works for reaching that goal.

Where's the Value?

The biggest mistake people make is leaving a message with zero value to the person receiving it. As I mentioned before, the prospect doesn't want to know how wonderful you are and a bunch of other blather about what you and your company do.

Think about this for a moment. Did the prospect wake up thinking about how great it would be if you called them? No, the prospect has things to do—that's the silver bullet you need to understand. Your message must contain a value statement that benefits the prospect. This means you need to summarize one key piece of information they will find of value in a single sentence.

Here's the text of what we would all agree is a poor, yet typical, voicemail I received:

"Hello, I'm looking for the person who is in charge of new customers. My name is John, and I'm with XYZ Company. We specialize in helping companies like yours increase their sales. We've been in business for more than fifteen years and have won numerous awards, which means the systems and methods we use work. Each time we work with a company, we are able to help them be more successful. What is even better is we have plans to fit all sizes of companies and budgets. We don't require lengthy contracts and we've found most of our customers like our thirty-day plans. Please have the person who is charge of finding new customers call me at "xxx-xxx-xxxx" extension "xxx" and ask for me, John.

The text does not do justice to how poorly this message sounded on the phone; and yes, I had to clean up the grammar to allow you to understand what he even said. Here are the reasons why the message was lousy and had zero chance of ever working:

First, it lacked energy. You will have to take my word on this one. If you're going to leave a voicemail, then you better be able to do it with energy. This person was not just *bad*; he was an embarrassment to the sales profession. It sounded like he had just rolled out of bed, because his voice had no strength.

Second, this salesperson ran his words and syllables together to the point I couldn't understand who he was or what company he was with. However, I admit that I couldn't care less who he was or what he was trying to sell because of how he presented himself. If only this person knew the number of times I had to listen to the voicemail message just so I could transcribe it properly for this book.

Third, the quality of the telephone equipment he was using was horrible! I have no idea what type of system he was using, but it was muffling his voice. I'm sure it would have sounded horrible had I answered the phone, but replaying it on my voicemail made it sound even worse.

Fourth, the message was way too long, and the message wasn't about me, the prospect.

Fifth, one of the first things he talked about was about how wonderful his company was and the awards the company had won. Ask me if I care? No!

Finally, he ended the call by giving a phone number and an extension only once! Even if I wanted to call him back, I'd have to listen to the message five times to understand the number because his voice and tone were so bad and he gave the number only once.

Basically, this person missed the mark on all the critical points I shared in the preceding chapter regarding how to use the telephone. It is amazing the number of bad voicemail messages I receive, and I'm sure you do too. Why would anyone leave a message that lacks any level of clarity and energy? You could have the best message in the world, but if you can't leave it clearly and with energy, then forget it—you're not going to get anywhere.

A great technique I suggest is to leave yourself a message and listen to it. Most people are amazed at what they hear when they listen to their own messages. Listening to yourself will allow you to hear a key mistake, such as speaking too quickly and running your company name into other words so a person unfamiliar with your company would have little clue as to who you are.

You Thought They Would Return Your Call?

Don't expect the prospect to call you back. That's right! Your single voicemail most likely won't be returned. Instead, view your message as one of a series of messages you'll use to reach your prospect across different mediums.

You might be wondering why I'm talking about frequency of voice-mails. The reason is simple: I want you to keep calling! Eventually, somebody will answer; and eventually, you will have the conversation you want. The best part is when you do finally get a person to answer the phone, they most likely will already know you because of the voicemail messages you've left. With each voicemail you leave, you're planting another seed in the mind of the prospect as to who you are and the value you can bring.

Your voicemail must contain something of value for the person receiving it. The message is not about you. That's the last thing they want to hear. Leaving a voicemail message with someone who was not looking for you to call them and then blathering on about how great you are is a recipe for huge failure. The only thing you'll succeed at is stroking your own ego, and along the way you'll go broke due to a lack of sales.

Your message must be of interest to the prospect. The best way to do this is to look for information the prospect has most likely not seen that you have been able to review. Sharing in a voicemail you have this type of information can give you critical leverage. This is the same approach you would use if they had answered the phone. Remember, the key with your voicemail is not to complete a sale; it's to engage them in a conversation over a period of time. That is why you share information they will value.

The significance of this approach is that most prospects view sales-people as being clueless about the prospect's industry. They see salespeople as self-serving. When you leave a voicemail that is *not* self-serving, but rather focused on the prospect, you stand apart from your competition.

Short Messages = Greater Impact

Keep your messages short! There are a lot of people who say the key is keeping the message to less than thirty seconds or even twenty seconds.

I say this is still way too long! Keep prospecting voicemails short; never more than eighteen seconds and preferably as short as twelve seconds. Yes, getting a message down to twelve to eighteen seconds is tough, but it can be done. I've taught this strategy to thousands of salespeople, and it works!

Only one thing happens to a lengthy message—it gets deleted! Even worse than being deleted is having the prospect remember it was *you* who left the lengthy message. Brevity with voicemail is key. You must be tight and concise with no wasted words, including your title! Do you think the other person cares you're a "vice president of the north-south district in the western region?"

Let's dig into the hows and whys of a good voicemail message. You should only say three things into a voicemail:

1. A tight greeting/introduction: *"Robert, this is Joe Washburn of Southern Mechanical."*
2. A call-to-action and reason for the call: *"I have new information regarding changes to the metro building codes. I would be happy to share this with you."*
3. An invitation to contact you: *"Robert, give me a call at 555-555-5555 and we can discuss. Again, this is Joe Washburn, 555-555-5555."*

Notice you should give your phone number twice as it makes it that much easier for the prospect to remember it. To change things up, you may want to give your phone number right at the start and again at the end. How many times have you had to listen to a message to get the phone number correct? By giving it twice, you're making it as easy as possible for the prospect to call you. Making this change is good when you've left the prospect multiple voicemails, as it allows them to hear that each one is not the same.

Getting your messages down to the twelve-to-eighteen second timeframe takes effort, but the flow becomes easy once you master it. Notice how I also stated the prospect's name twice, but didn't use valuable time stating their last name. I want to keep things casual, and using a person's last name makes it too formal and eats up precious time. Finally, never forget what you said in the voicemail message.

Make detailed notes in your CRM system, because the last thing you want to do is have the person return your call and you not remember what you called them about.

Following are a few examples of topics you might use. Yes, they are specific to certain industries, but they should begin to give you ideas on how you can customize something for your industry.

1. If I sell insurance, I might leave a value statement saying something about how I have new information from an employee survey showing how employee attitudes toward insurance have changed.
2. If I sell computer services to businesses. I could say something with regard to a new study showing how companies are spending less on computer hardware due to changes in how they use what they have.

The idea is to not detail what you do and how great your company is in the value statement you leave with the prospect. The objective is to share one sentence that lets them know you have something of value that could help them.

Using voicemail as part of your prospecting campaign is not a license to leave the same exact message twice with the same person. This is an insult because you need to always assume the person heard the first message and chose not to respond. I feel insulted when a salesperson leaves me a duplicate message, to the point that I will never take the time to connect with them regardless of what they might have to offer.

Is There an Energy Shortage?

Remember, the objective of the voicemail message is to get the prospect to see you as a person with whom they would want to connect and do business. The last thing anyone wants is to do business with a person who comes across as lethargic. Energy sells, because it conveys passion and confidence. Remember the example I shared earlier in this chapter? Yes, too much energy can come across as cheesy and artificial, but that is hardly ever going to happen with 99.5 percent of all salespeople.

Customers and prospects want to feel confident about the salespeople they encounter, which means you must display confidence in yourself as a salesperson.

There are three things you can do to convey energy and confidence. I mentioned these earlier, but I want to repeat them because of their importance:

1. Use a headset to make your calls. Engaging people talk with their hands, and that's pretty hard to do when you have one hand holding the handset.
2. Stand up when making your prospecting calls. Standing up brings more oxygen to your lungs, and it's amazing how much stronger your voice will sound.
3. Practice your messages. The first prospecting call you make each day should be to yourself to simply get yourself in gear. It's no different than athletes warming up before a game. Practicing out loud also gives you the chance to make sure you know what you're going to say. It's amazing how a little preparation can and will increase your level of confidence.

What about the argument that some people just don't check their messages? Yes, there are people like that, and the challenge is we don't always know who that person is until after we've left multiple messages. There have been plenty of articles and studies that say the younger a person, the less likely they are to check voicemail. I tend to agree, but that's still no reason to downplay the role voicemail can play in a prospecting strategy. My philosophy: I will leave a prospect a voicemail and continue to use voicemail as *one* of my prospecting tools with the person until I've been told by him or her to not use it. As with so many things, it's easy to make a quick assumption and then wind up having that quick assumption be proven wrong.

ELEVEN RULES FOR LEAVING A GREAT VOICEMAIL

1. Only include three things: a greeting, a call to action, and contact information.

2. Never let your voicemail go longer than eighteen seconds and strive to keep it as close to twelve seconds as possible. This means you need to practice—first to know what you're saying, and second to be able to say it clearly to allow the other party to understand what you're saying.

3. Give the prospect information they will value and want to receive. When you're leaving your message, make sure you leave a short statement (a call to action) about a key report or bit of information you will be happy to share with them when they call back.

4. State your message with confidence and a full voice. Nothing will kill a prospecting call faster than a weak message. Stand up, focus, and be deliberate with your words.

5. State your phone number twice and say it slowly! It is important to give your phone number twice, and be sure to enunciate each digit. You may know what you're saying, but your prospect doesn't.

6. Do not leave your website address or say when you're available. Knowing your website gives them a way to find out about you without having to call you back. Same thing goes for asking them to call you back at a certain time. It's your job to be available for the prospect. It's not the prospect's job to be available for you.

7. Use a headset to allow you to speak with your hands. We always speak with more energy when our hands are free.

8. Note in your CRM what message you left so you never leave the same message twice. By recording the details of the message, you will be prepared should the prospect call back.

9. Leave your subsequent messages on different days of the week and different times of the day. If somebody is busy Tuesday at two in the afternoon one week, there's a good chance they will be busy the following Tuesday at two in the afternoon. Rotate your days and your times.

10. Use the person's first name twice. We all like hearing our own name. But don't waste valuable time saying their last name; business today is not that formal.

11. Use voicemail along with other prospecting tools. Some people simply do not ever check their voicemail. The last thing you want to do is leave someone message after message, and nothing ever happens. Make sure your prospecting strategy includes multiple techniques.

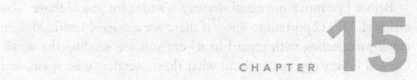

Email, Communication, and Connection

I bet this is one of the first chapters many people turn to after buying this book. Let's not kid ourselves; everyone wants to think email is the best way to prospect. The number one prospecting question I receive from salespeople is how to get people to open and respond to emails. What I ask them in return is a question I pose to you: why are you placing so much emphasis on email? Yes, it can be efficient, but it also can become the lazy person's way to prospect. Far too many salespeople use the excuse that email is the only way to reach prospects. I'll tell you why salespeople say this. It's because they don't want to have to work, and they're scared of actually having to pick up the telephone!

Before you send one more prospecting email, take the time to develop an overall strategic and tactical plan for how you will go forward. The easiest approach is to split your contact frequency between phone calls and email: one-half phone calls and one-half emails. If you're in an industry where social media is prevalent, then you can go one-third on each: email, telephone, and social media. (I will discuss this more in a later chapter.) Sending emails by themselves is a waste of time. Worse yet, you could wind up getting your email address pegged as spam, never to be seen again by a prospect regardless of what you say. The content you use in an email is content you can use in a phone call; just remember to not mirror it 100 percent. The last thing you want to be seen as is a lazy salesperson who sends the same information using different methods.

Before I go into more email strategy, it's time for one of those "disclaimers." It's important to know if there are any legal restrictions on email prospecting with regard to where you are sending the email. Canada is very aggressive about what they consider to be spam, and the consequences can be severe. Canada is not alone, as there are other countries with email regulations of varying degrees. My advice is first to not do anything that breaks a law. No exceptions. Second, ignorance is not a valid defense in not knowing what you can or cannot do. I agree there can be gray areas with regard to what is a business email and what is a personal email and if it is classified as legal or illegal. Whatever you send, do so with complete integrity, assuring what you're doing conforms to the regulatory environment in which you're sending the email.

Many of you reading this book may also work in an industry governed by various regulations to which you must adhere. Many times the regulations require a disclaimer at the end of each email or state rules over what can or cannot be put into an email. My philosophy is to always adhere to whatever regulations pertain to your industry.

Your Toolbox Needs More Than One Tool

It's not that email is a terrible prospecting tool. It's a fantastic tool when used for the right reasons, and I do use it all the time. Just remember it's only *one* of your prospecting tools. Unfortunately because it's so easy to use, too many salespeople use it too much.

I want to make my prospecting process so effective I don't have to rely solely on one piece of software to determine if I make commission. The biggest problem that exists with regard to email is the mass blast email campaigns far too many people rely on. Just because you sent one hundred emails, why should you think one hundred people would even get them, let alone read them?

I interact with talented people from all areas of the sales world, and I will tell you there are no two people who embrace identical strategies or philosophies when it comes to emailing prospects. There are simply too many different combinations and variables that salespeople must consider. In this chapter, I'm going to provide you with numerous strategies. I'm going to break down the reasons why various email strategies don't work and, then show you ones you can use effectively.

Please do not think this is the only chapter you need to read in this book. If you do, don't come back to me in a few months or a few years and say the prospecting strategies I shared didn't work. Using email as your sole prospecting strategy is simply not going to work, period! You might find it works for a short time, but to think it can work for you year after year is, in my opinion, stupid and a reflection of your own laziness. Yes, I'm being blunt, but it's my mission to get those of you who think email is the answer to quit thinking that.

You Mean You Didn't Read My Email?

First, you need to accept that your prospect may not even have seen your email, because their spam filter may have blocked it. This often is the direct result of a salesperson who thinks they will reach a person by sending a blitz of emails over a short period of time. Sending more than three or four emails to the same person in a thirty-day period when they don't even know you is asking the spam/junk filters to exile you forever.

Second, just because you wrote your email on your computer doesn't mean the prospect is going to see it on a computer. Chances are they'll view it on their smartphone. And even if they do that, whether they read it or delete it will be based on the subject line.

Today there are as many barriers to reaching someone via email as there are barriers to reaching someone on the phone; it's just that we don't see the email barriers. I'll dig into this more later, but I want you to begin embracing the concept that email works as a prospecting tool when the message is tight, short, and beneficial to the person receiving it. Your objective is to assess the role email plays in your prospecting process and use it wisely as *one* of your tools, not the only tool.

This Is Not the Time for a Shopping List

One time in the course of a one-week period I received at least five prospecting emails that were nothing more than shopping lists from the same person. When I say "shopping lists," I mean the emails listed a variety of services the salesperson thought I should buy. When I see a list like that, all I think is, "How could somebody be so stupid to think that approach might work?"

How could an email that includes a list of things possibly be effective, especially if the sender has zero relationship with the person to whom they are sending the email? If you're sending prospecting emails that are nothing more than a shopping list, stop immediately. You're just wasting your time. If you're thinking about using this approach, save yourself some brainpower and stop. Even if you did get a response back from the other person asking you for information or even a price, I'll bet in 95 percent of those situations all they're doing is comparing you against someone else. Sending a shopping list as your email strategy is an open invitation for the prospect to use you to help them shop for a better deal. I say this because I've had numerous professional buyers tell me they do it whenever they're in need of a quick second or third quote. If you want to spend your sales career helping your competition, have at it, but don't get mad when you don't make your numbers.

Components of a Strong Email

Prospecting emails can be effective if you use them as one component of your prospecting plan. The key is to keep your emails tight and focused on what will interest or benefit the other person. My suggestion is no more than three paragraphs containing two sentences each. This allows you to convey a single idea without the fluff and garbage prospects don't want to see.

Before you even think about sending a prospecting email, ask yourself these four questions:

- ▶ Does my email have a call to action?
- ▶ Does it carry a benefit the receiver can relate to?
- ▶ Does it have a personal connection with the receiver?
- ▶ Is it time-sensitive?

If you have spent any amount of time in the direct mail industry, you will recognize these questions as the basic elements of a direct mail letter. The problem I see today is too many salespeople, because of their laziness or ineptitude, believe they can simply throw emails out like snowflakes. They think if they cover enough people, they'll be successful. Well, as the old saying goes, even a blind squirrel will find an acorn occasionally. You might get lucky once, but you'll never be lucky enough to make your numbers.

Use the questions I listed previously to help you write your content. Most importantly, don't think merely sending a bunch of emails will garner you success. No, the best sales prospecting letter is supported by an integrated campaign that includes phone calls and a web presence. This is the big reason I believe ninety-nine percent of all email prospecting campaigns do not work—they are not integrated with other prospecting tools.

Is Your Subject Line Working for You or Against You?

Your subject line is basically the headline of your email. The same concept that applies to a news headline applies to your email subject line— the objective is to pique interest and get the recipient to read more. If the subject line doesn't grab your prospect's attention, it doesn't matter how good your email is because the prospect won't read it.

Your first obstacle is to make sure your subject line (or for that matter, any other part of the email) doesn't contain something spam filters would likely block. If you're looking for a list of words, sorry, but I don't have them. And I'll argue neither does anybody else, despite what they might say. In my job I have the opportunity to speak to and work with many of the largest corporations in the world, and a topic that comes up a lot is their own email systems. I've had people from some of the largest companies share with me that their company email filters even block emails from their spouses or kids. To think anyone can figure out the perfect list of words is crazy and, even if they could come up with such a list, it would be outdated tomorrow. My view is the same line Google has used for years, "Don't be evil."

The key is to deliver a subject line that will compel the person receiving the email to actually open it. When developing your subject line, putting anything in it about yourself is the kiss of death. It might inflate your ego, but it will do nothing else. What I have found works is to keep the subject line simple and short. You want your recipient to be interested enough to read the first few words—especially if they are flipping through email messages on a handheld device.

Here are some of my recommendations for what to include in a subject line:

- ▶ Name of an association the person you're emailing is involved with
- ▶ Name of a regulatory agency or government body that has an impact on them
- ▶ Name of a person the recipient of the email respects
- ▶ Name of a product or division from another company in their industry or in their community
- ▶ Date and name of a specific event the person would recognize

Please note: the subject line you use must fit the topic of the email. Bait and switch is highly unethical. It pains me to have to write this disclaimer, but we've all been on the receiving end of emails like that.

Don't Lose Me Now

The opening sentence of your email should contain words like *strategic*, *value*, *leadership*, *profit*, *trust*, *leverage*, *advantage*, and *competitive*. The only way to know for sure which words work best for you is to try different words. Words and sentences that work well for one industry may not work well in another.

Getting a prospect to open your email is only the first step in email marketing. Your opening sentence must also set the tone and give them a reason to keep reading. This is also where you have to discard all of the rules you learned in school about how to write a letter. Taking the first paragraph to introduce yourself and your company and going on to state how much of a privilege it is to be sending the email isn't going to gain you a prospect. Yes, it pains me to say this, considering my mother was an English major in college and taught grammar for more than thirty years. One of the best ways to craft a prospecting email is to think you're writing a tweet or texting someone. You have to write succinctly in order to grab attention.

Before digging into specifically what works, let's start with what doesn't work. Do not use an opening line or phrase like any of these:

> My name is . . .
>
> I work for . . .
>
> My company does . . .
>
> We've helped . . .
>
> We're responsible for . . .

Want to know what is wrong with those? They are about the sender. They scream, "I'm trying to sell you something!" It's a horrible first impression and it looks like every other email. If you learn only one thing regarding email from this book, I hope it is this: prospecting is not about you! It's about them.

So how do you start an email? Consider the strategies that follow.

STRATEGY 1: Leverage a Recognizable Interest

The most common recognizable point is a referral or familiar name, but there are so many more! Examples include an industry event, competitor, acquisition, annual or quarterly report, press release, award or recognition, or promotion. Whatever you choose, make sure it's something important to your prospect. Here are some examples of how to begin a first sentence:

> Your recent acquisition of ABC Corporation . . .
>
> The FDA has released its new findings . . .
>
> Last night the city council passed the ordinance on . . .
>
> In a new study, the AMA . . .
>
> Update on the research regarding . . .

New numbers are out updating . . . .

UBC revised standards state . . .

Examples specific to B2C might include:

Building code changes . . .

Financial goals . . .

College funding . . .

Goals for retirement . . .

The Green Bay Packers this year . . .

The University of Texas announced . . .

STRATEGY 2: Promote Industry Expertise

People are so busy today just getting through their daily routines. They no longer have the luxury of staying current on industry knowledge like they once did. Your role as an industry expert can be invaluable to your prospects, so you need to flaunt that expertise. When something changes in the industry—whether it affects their business role, is regulatory in nature, is an upcoming business event, or is a competitive landscape change—don't assume they already know about it. The mere fact that you can show them you are an expert allows you to stand out.

An example of an industry expert first sentence may look like this:

In the past 18 months, there has been an enormous shift in . . .

The new codes are stricter than expected . . .

With the EU predicting a change, we see . . .

Industry changes impacting competitors . . .

B2C examples include:

New building codes don't require as much . . .

Retirement planning models we've seen . . .

Assessing risk requires expertise . . .

Looking closely at these examples, you might say they're similar to those in the first strategy—and you're right, they are. The more the opening sentences can incorporate not just one strategy, but two or even three, the greater the probability you will be successful in prompting the prospect to read and respond to your email.

STRATEGY 3: Use Strategic Words

Clearly your company is in business to alleviate a pain or create some sort of benefit. The challenge is that so are a whole bunch of other companies and salespeople, and standing out is mission critical for you to be successful. Creating value is the easiest way to do that.

Depending upon your audience, there are some keywords that can elevate your business vocabulary to match your target recipient. Strong B2B words you can leverage around your topic are *strategic, value, leadership, profit, trust, leverage, advantage* and *competitive.*

Here are some good examples in action:

Your Q4 profits are in line to leverage X, which would strategically . . .

Leadership changes at several key positions. . .

Changes in the competitive landscape . . .

Selling in a B2C environment allows you to use some of the same words, but many are different. The best words I've found include *security, safety, trust, confidence, current,* and *value.*

A few examples for B2C include:

Safety must always be the #1 issue. . .

Creating confidence is not something that comes easily. . .

Changes in current value will put more strategies at risk. . .

Email Scripts You Need

What does a great prospecting email look like? It does not include any graphics or attachments and is only four to six sentences in length, broken into two to three paragraphs. That's it! A prospecting email is not the place for a three-thousand-word detailed analysis of what you can do. The objective of a prospecting email is to create a level of interest to give you the opportunity to have a future discussion with the prospect.

To help make the email easy to read on a handheld device, always double-space the paragraphs.

Keep your signature line simple. Do not include your company logo or awards you've won. If your company requires you have a detailed signature line with the company logo, then you should have an alternate signature line you use when prospecting.

Here's the signature line I use for my emails:

> Mark Hunter "The Sales Hunter"
> 402-445-2110
> www.TheSalesHunter.com

Some will argue I should not include my website. The guideline I use is if you are with a small company, include your website. If you work for a well-known company, do not include your URL, but rather have the name of your company in plain text.

Now it's time to see all these tips put together. Here is an example of an ideal prospecting email:

> **Subject:** New Fed. Regulations Released
>
> The federal government has updated regulations, and companies will now have 18 months to comply. The changes are quite extensive, although there are ways to comply without disrupting business.
>
> We have new information I would be happy to share with you. Here at Brown Consulting, we've been monitoring this situation closely.

Call me at 555-555-5555 and I'll be happy to share the
information with you, so you can avoid any compliance issues.
Randy, thanks and I look forward to talking with you.

Mark Hunter
Brown Consulting
555-555-5555

This example is mobile friendly, six sentences, three paragraphs, and
all about what will interest the prospect. Is it going to get a 100 percent
response rate? No, but I bet it will get a far higher response than other
emails you've been using.

Here are three more examples:

Subject: Building Code Changes

Beginning this month, new building code changes have taken
effect. Changes are significant and upgrades are required.

We have insights we can share with you to help you through
this process. Please call or email, and I will be happy to discuss
further.

Mark Hunter
Acme Engineering
555-555-5555

Subject: Profitable Sales Growth

Discounting to close sales is becoming a major problem for
many salespeople. The impact on profit from discounting can be
significant.

We have some quick ways to ensure discounting is not necessary
and would be happy to share them with you. Feel free to call or
email and we can discuss further.

Mark Hunter "The Sales Hunter"
402-445-2110
www.TheSalesHunter.com

Subject: College Tuition Support

Getting everything in place for college is difficult for many families. There are new federal guidelines regarding how to apply for tuition support and I would be happy to share them with you.

Feel free to call or email me at your convenience and I can share with you several ways to make it easier to complete the paperwork.

Ross Johnson
Johnson Financial Services
555-555-5555

If I Send It, Will They See It?

If you asked me what days are best to send a prospecting email, I would say Tuesday, Wednesday, or Thursday—but there are plenty of exceptions to the rule. Each industry has its own business cycle. I work with industries where the only day you can reach someone is on a Monday, and other industries where it can be any day *but* Monday. The key is to experiment, keeping notes all along. It's amazing that not only the day of the week can make a difference, but also the time of the year.

When sending more than one email to the same person, make sure you alter the day and time of the week. Most people adhere to the same schedule week in and week out, and that means you need to vary the days and times you send your emails if you want to have a better probability of the prospect responding. Some people who rarely respond to a prospecting email may suddenly be drawn to respond when they receive it at 5:30 p.m. or 6:15 a.m. Experiment and find what works best for your target audience.

Don't pepper anyone! By this I mean don't send anyone the same email twice, thinking they didn't see it the first time. Also, don't send email after email, thinking they have to at least open one of them. Sending too many emails to a person in too short of a timeframe is a great way to get picked off by spam filters. My preference is to never send more than four emails to a person in a six-week period before backing off, if they have not responded to you. I back off for ninety days, and then will do like it says on the back of shampoo bottles: "Repeat."

Don't Let a Smartphone Keep You From Looking Smart

A huge mistake far too many salespeople make is spending hours on their laptops or desktops crafting the perfect emails. After writing them, they look at them and marvel at how smart they are and how the emails are going to generate the responses they want. They begin dreaming of success, as if they had just won the lottery and a marching band is about to enter their rooms, followed by the media with cameras rolling as a giant lottery check is presented. Dream on! It simply is not going to happen, because of a huge mistake few salespeople realize.

You probably wrote your prospecting email on a large screen, either a laptop or desktop, and to you the email visually looks and reads great. The problem is your prospect will most likely see it on a small screen, primarily their smartphone or tablet. One of the best things you can do after writing a prospecting email is send it to yourself and view it on your phone. When I'm sharing this concept with sales teams, I will often ask them to take out their smartphones, open up their email, and compare how their email looks on their devices with other people around them. Even within the same company and similar devices, emails can and will look different due to each person's personal settings. Failing to know how your email is going to appear on a handheld device is sheer stupidity. With the broad array of devices used today, the likelihood of your email appearing less than stellar should always be a concern.

There is a second issue that comes along with emails read on small screens: the level of focus your email receives when viewed on a handheld device. Ask yourself, "Do I spend more time looking at each individual email when I'm viewing them on my laptop or desktop compared to my smartphone?" Most likely your answer is "Yes." I don't have any vetted data to back up my theory, other than the responses I've received from thousands of salespeople I've asked in meetings over the years who have said, "Yes, I'm less focused when viewing email on a smartphone, and I'm more likely to delete the emails."

Many people, myself included, prefer checking email on a smart-phone. When I use my smartphone to check email, the only thing I'm seeing is a couple of words in the subject line and maybe the first one hundred characters of the email. Based on those two items, as well as who sent it, I make a quick decision to delete or read the email. More than likely, I will delete it. We tend to go through our email much faster when checking it on our smartphones versus when working on our lap-tops. This is why I stress the importance of the subject line and the first sentence.

Lest you think the subject line and first few words are all you need to focus upon, let me say, "No, there's even more." Let's say you received an email from me, and the subject line and first couple of words were intriguing, so you opened it up to read it. If it's a lengthy email with graphics and attachments, it may never load properly. You will likely delete it without reading it. This is why I can't stress enough to follow the criteria outlined in this chapter about the ideal length of a prospecting email.

Every idea I've shared in this chapter on how to use email as a pros-pecting tool is to help you get past the issue I've come to call "smartphone deletion frenzy." I can't tell you the number of comments I've received back from people with whom I've shared this issue. Each person has said that by making their emails "smartphone friendly," they've been able to connect with people they were not able to reach previously.

Ten Rules for Using Email to Prospect

1. Use email as one prospecting strategy. Email is not the only prospecting tool. Relying 100 percent on it will only result in problems arising with obstacles like email filters. "Best prac-tice" prospecting is when you use email as only one of the prospecting tools.
2. Write the email to be read on a smartphone. A high per-centage of emails are viewed on a smartphone. So, your email must be as easy to read on a smartphone as it is to read on a laptop.
3. Keep it short. It should be no more than six sentences and no more than two to three paragraphs. The prospect is less likely

to read long emails and even less likely to engage with you if the email is long.

4. Include no attachments or graphics. Keep your email clean to allow it to load quickly regardless of the device being used and to give spam filters one less reason to potentially block your email.

5. Never send the same email twice to the same person. Always assume the person has read your email. Sending the same message twice is telling the customer you don't trust them.

6. Include a compelling subject line. People are looking for a reason to delete rather than read. Failing to give them a subject line they will find of interest is inviting a high non-open rate.

7. Focus on the first one hundred characters of the email, which are extremely important. Since such a high number of emails are viewed on a smartphone, it's important to ensure what is seen initially is as powerful as possible.

8. Never send more than three to four emails in a six-week period without receiving a response. This minimizes the likelihood of the email being tagged as spam by their email filters. The specific factors used will vary dramatically, but being banished to the spam or junk folder is not something you want to risk.

9. Do not make the email a shopping list of everything you can do. Each email you send must be focused around one specific point. Turning your email into a shopping list is putting too much in front of the lead or prospect at once.

10. Use email-tracking software to monitor key emails to see if they were opened. The best email is useless if you don't know if it's been even opened and read.

CHAPTER 16

Referrals and Other Major Pipeline Builders

ompanies must select new vendors, whether to provide something new or to replace an existing vendor, on a regular basis. A few years ago, my company did a vendor review to determine if we should move to a new website design and hosting company. We believed the service of our current web company was up to standards, but until we looked at options we couldn't be certain. We went through the review process and ultimately chose to remain with our current vendor.

Fast forward to today and we're in the process of switching vendors, based on the quality of the work we've seen from a web company one of our business associates has used. I've watched for some time the quality of work they do, and in conversations with my business associate I have learned how pleased he has been with this company. The process of switching began with me contacting the vendor. That's a shame—the vendor could have landed the business several years earlier if they had only reached out to me. The problem was they didn't know I existed, because they never bothered to ask my business associate for referrals.

I share this situation because it hits close to home with too many salespeople and customers. I was in a situation where my current vendor wasn't doing anything *wrong* to warrant me dropping them, but they also weren't doing anything awesome. Put another way, there wasn't enough pain or gain to warrant a move. This is where salespeople drop the ball. If only the web company my business associate was using had taken the time to ask for referrals (which I know my business associate would have been happy to give!), it could have reached out to me several years sooner. They would have had an additional client, and I would have been receiving better support.

Why Aren't You Asking?

Most salespeople are hesitant to ask for referrals. I believe it's due to a lack of confidence in how the customer might respond. The salesperson isn't just concerned they won't get the referral, but also that merely asking for the referral will damage the relationship they have with the customer. The salesperson choosing to forgo the referral process is making a major mistake, as they don't benefit from what the process has to offer.

Asking for referrals does several things for the salesperson. Naturally, the biggest is the salesperson gains access to high-potential prospects, but asking for referrals also helps strengthen the salesperson's relationship with the customer. When you ask a current customer for a referral, the customer has a choice: they can either give you a referral or say "no." Sure, there are variations on both, but to keep things simple, it comes down to a yes or no. Regardless of how they answer, they first have to think about the relationship they have with you. The simple action of the customer having to think about the relationship they have with you is huge. I've found on numerous occasions when I've asked my own clients for referrals, it winds up creating additional conversations about how working with me has benefited the customer. Think about this for a moment. The customer winds up making positive comments about you and your company, which end up strengthening the feelings they have toward you.

Each time I've asked for a referral, I have come away a better and more productive salesperson. Do I ask all of my clients for referrals? No. Let's put the cards on the table. I have had some customers I've never asked for referrals. In these instances, the reason was the profile of the customer led me to believe that any referral they would give me would likely not fit the profile of the prospect I sought. The worst thing you can do is ask for a referral and then not maximize it. Years ago I met Roger, who was a dynamic life insurance agent. He was without a doubt a class act. The first time I met him, he blew me away with how much he already knew about me and even what my expectations were. I came to rely on him, as his advice was spot-on and everything he said and did exuded confidence and trust. Roger found me through a referral from another person. He was open about his desire for referrals, and over the course of several years working with him I gave him a number of them. It was easy to give him referrals, because I trusted him and I wanted others to benefit from his expertise, too.

Since meeting Roger, I have never encountered another person who used referrals as efficiently as he does. Roger was incredibly successful with referrals for three reasons. First, he did a great job taking care of his customers. Second, he knew when to ask for referrals. Third, he was always appreciative of referrals and kept everybody in the know regarding how he was handling them.

The Four-Step Dance

Just because the example I used is a B2C, don't think for a moment you can't leverage referrals in a B2B environment. You can! The steps are exactly the same. The activity of asking and leveraging referrals comes down to four simple steps. The steps are so easy, and I believe they will make you as much money as, or more than, any other strategy in this book. There is nothing complicated about any one of the steps; you simply must be disciplined enough to carry them out.

FOUR-STEP REFERRAL DEVELOPMENT

1. Ask for referrals. Every time the customer sees value in what you're selling is a time when you should ask for a referral.
2. Connect with the referral. Ideally, the person who gives you the name will connect the two of you through an email or phone call. Even if that is not the case, following up as soon as possible is showing respect to the person who referred you.
3. Keep the person who gave you the referral in the loop. Don't keep the person who gave you the referral in the dark. By

keeping them in the loop, you will encourage them to provide you with more referrals.

4. Be appreciative each step along the way. Nothing you do will create more referrals along the way than showing appreciation to each person in the process.

STEP 1: Ask for Referrals

To become good (and when I say "good," I mean really good), you must make asking for referrals part of your selling process. Financial planners and those in a B2C environment tend to be better at this, but as I said earlier, the process is the same for B2B and the rewards can be just as great.

Ask for a referral any time your customer has seen value in what you provide. Yes, that is typically going to be after you've sold them, but don't think that is the only time. Many times in B2B sales, the selling process can extend over a long period of time. Use the periods where the customer sees value in what you provide as an opportunity to ask. For example, say you come out of a productive meeting with your customer regarding your proposal, and the customer has complimented you on what you've shown. Asking at that time for somebody in another division or operating unit to whom you should talk is certainly appropriate. You'll either find yourself with a name, or they won't provide one—either way, they will respect you for your confidence. The only time I would not ask is if the sale you're working on is so significant to both your company and your customer that maintaining one hundred percent focus is not just expected, but essential.

Ask for a referral immediately after gaining an order. This is the most natural time, but even at this phase it's amazing how few salespeople actually do it. The fact that we as a sales community do not ask for referrals after each sale says a lot about the lack of confidence many salespeople have in what they do.

Ask for a referral within a set period of time after the customer has bought from you. The nice thing with this is that not only can *you* do this, but your customer service people can, too. Many times during the start up, installation, and/or early days of the sale, your customer service team is more involved with the customer than you are. Coach the customer service people to ask for referrals. It's always interesting how many times an unassuming customer service person can gain an amazing number of leads and referrals.

Have an annual schedule you follow to ensure that someone from the sales team follows up with all customers to gain referrals. It's easy to forget about asking the good customer you've had for years for referrals. By having a dedicated time or process, you will be far less likely to let the good customer slide off your referral radar screen.

For customers who are buying from you on a regular basis and with whom you have regular communication, asking for referrals must be an activity you do regularly. My suggestion is that you intentionally ask every six months, or any other time you're with the customer and the conversation lends itself to asking.

KEEP IT SIMPLE

The art of asking for a referral is keeping it simple. The best approach I've found is wrapping the request around one of two things: either ask for a referral as you confirm a key benefit the customer values, or ask when you are seeking overall feedback on you and your company. Here are three examples that you can use to develop an approach that works for you and your industry.

> "You mentioned how much you appreciate the way we are helping
> to automate your systems. I suspect you know other businesses that
> would benefit in the same way you do, right?"

Notice how in my question, I made the assumption the person knows others. It's amazing how by merely crafting your sentence using an assumptive approach, you can generate referrals.

> "How is our new system working for you? I'm thinking you're already
> seeing the value in it. I'm sure you know of others who would benefit
> in the same way. Who pops into your mind?"

This second example allows for the customer to share with you any number of things that ultimately will help you ensure you're meeting their expectations. The beauty is you are achieving two things: meeting their expectations and gaining referrals.

> "It's great how we've been able to build a plan that allows your family to achieve the financial goals you've wanted for so long. Would you know other families that would benefit from similar plans?"

The important thing is to not overcomplicate it. Keep it simple, so it becomes a regular part of a conversation you have with customers.

STEP 2: Connect with the Referral

Your best way to connect with the referral is by having the person giving you the referral personally connect the two of you. There are some people who will say the best approach is to make the request to connect the two of you as part of the initial request for a referral. Personally, I don't like that approach, as it can come across as asking too much of the customer at one time. My feeling is one of the reasons salespeople don't ask for more referrals is because they believe you have to ask for the connection at the same time as the initial ask. It is possible, though, for these two actions to happen separately.

When you do ask for the connection, make it easy. After the customer has given you the name of somebody, thank them and then ask what in particular they feel the referral would like best about what you offer. This now makes the customer feel important, because you're asking for their input. After they've shared with you what they feel the person to whom they are referring you will like best, then take the time to ask if they will make a personal introduction. How they make the introduction is up to them, and I will always default to what the customer prefers. Typically it tends to be an email introduction, but just as often it is a phone call, social media message, text, or face-to-face meeting. The key is to ask them to do it and, at the same time, to get the referral's contact information. I will say that with the level of resources available via the Internet, it's not too hard to locate anyone's contact information, but getting it from the customer is still the best approach.

When the customer gives you a name, it is absolutely essential, regardless of how the introduction is made, to ask for their permission to use their name (if they are not willing to make the introduction themselves). If they say you can't use their name, I'll leave it up to you to determine if the referral has merit or is simply a name they're throwing out to keep you happy. Regardless of how your conversation goes regarding referrals, you must show appreciation to the person. One way to show appreciation is by asking how *you* can help *them*. It might be giving them a referral. If it is, make sure to not just give them any referral you can think of quickly just to return the favor. No, your objective is to go above and beyond.

STEP 3: Keep the Person Who Gave You the Referral Up to Date

This is easy and fun, yet despite this I'm amazed at the number of salespeople who ask for referrals but never follow up to keep people informed. The person who gave you the referral went out of their way to do it. Don't you think you owe them the respect of keeping them informed? Yes! Not only is it the right thing to do, but it's also amazing how it will wind up creating more referrals for you.

How you choose to follow up is going to depend on the industry you're in and people's preferred methods of communication. The only rule I have is to make sure how you communicate back to the person who gave you the referral is by using the communication method they prefer most.

STEP 4: Be Appreciative Each Step Along the Way

This isn't so much a separate step as it is a guiding principle used throughout each part of the prospecting process. Remember, the way you treat the person who made the referral to you will go a long way in determining if you get more referrals from the original person, not to mention the person referred to you. As long as you remember to treat others the way your mother taught you, you'll do just fine.

Salespeople always ask me if they should compensate the people who give them referrals in some manner. Minimally, you should send a handwritten note. Whether it includes a gift is your call, based on your industry, company policy, the competitive marketplace, etc. The variables are too great for me to say what's right, but I definitely believe you can't go wrong with showing some appreciation.

Borrowing from the Best

Use anniversaries as a great way to gain new leads. This is a method financial planners and insurance agents use very well, but I contend it works for all industries. The process is simple: use the anniversary of when the customer first began working with you as a reason to call and thank them for their business, and follow it by asking for a referral.

A few years back, I was consulting with a regional bank and an approach we put in place was to call customers on both the commercial and personal sides of the business every six months. The objective of the call was to first gain referrals, but it also allowed the bank to gather feedback on its services, as well as sell additional products and services. The results were better than they had ever had on any other telephone sales initiative. The bank gained three ways. First, they received referrals. Second, the conversation with the customer many times went further, and the banker was able to provide the customer with additional products. Third, the banker occasionally would reach a customer who was not pleased with the service they had received, but didn't think it was bad enough to actually contact customer service. This unhappy customer possibly would have gone undetected and moved to another bank if the bank hadn't put in place a method to call current customers for referrals. Once the problems were revealed, it gave the bank the opportunity to address them and fix them, likely preventing the customer from taking their business to a competitor.

Blitz, Blitz, and Blitz Again

This approach is one I've had the privilege of putting in place in a wide number of companies across numerous industries in both B2B and B2C. Each time I first presented it I was met with skepticism, but without fail, each company that has used the process has been able to significantly increase their number of referrals and leads.

The approach is not difficult. The number one requirement is blocking time on the calendar far enough in advance to ensure there is time to make it happen. As the subtitle says, it's a blitz. You contact each of your existing customers during three specific periods of time each year. Each contact is for a different reason. Here is what this looks like:

February/March: Referral Request

July/August: Customer Feedback

November/December: Appreciation

In February or March, contact all of your accounts and simply say, "Here at _____, we're having a referral blitz, and I'm contacting each of my accounts to ask them for the names of others who I might be able to talk with." The approach is straightforward and works surprisingly well. When customers are told upfront what the salesperson wants, they often are more appreciative and helpful than if the salesperson beats around the bush while asking for something.

The next round of blitzing occurs in July or August. When you contact each of your customers this time, you focus on thanking them for their business and asking them about your company's level of customer service. Your objective here is to get them to realize the quality you provide them and, in so doing, to get them to talk about it. Immediately after you thank them for their comments, ask them for the names of others who would benefit from the same service.

Your final round of lead blitzing occurs in the November/December timeframe. Again, you contact each customer. The focus this time is purely to network and wish them the best for the holidays (depending on when exactly you call them). Many times calls during this time of year will become more personal and conversational, as people tend to be more relaxed. Don't forget to use calls at this time of year to find out their plans for the upcoming year. Again, this is an opportunity to ask the person with whom you are talking for the names of companies and individuals who also could benefit from what you offer.

Keeping your pipeline full is essential. More important than just keeping the pipeline full is keeping it full with high-potential leads. This is why I like tapping into existing customers for leads. Asking for referrals is one of the most efficient ways to gain new customers. Never stop believing in what you do and the benefit you provide your customers. Why would anyone give you a referral if they felt you didn't believe in what you're selling? At the same time, one of the best ways to increase your confidence is by having the raving customer give you the names of other people to contact.

My own goal when it comes to referrals is to always gain at least one new lead from each existing customer. Does this keep my pipeline full? No, but it gives me more than I would have otherwise.

CHAPTER 17

The Value and Pitfalls of Social Media

I f you listen to the news, you would believe social media sites are taking over the world. It's inescapable, and let's admit, we've all watched more than one cat video or "stupid stunt gone bad" video. I continue to be amazed at the millions of views such things garner in just a few days. The wide number of ways people use social media sites to earn a living also amazes me. All of this leaves me wondering what makes some things wildly successful on the Internet, while the vast majority of content fades away, never to be seen again? Let me answer the question by asking two more questions:

▶ Would you build a home on land you didn't own?
▶ Would you build a home on land you rented, but the landlord could change the agreement terms at any time?

What are your answers? I suspect you would say "no" to both those questions. There is no way I would ever build a house on land I didn't own or on land where the terms of the agreement could change at any moment. I doubt you would, either. Yet, this is exactly what people do when they say they're going all-in on using social media sites to develop leads and customers.

Anyone who has been in the social media space for some time has seen how the owners of these sites can and will change the rules. What makes it frustrating is they tend to *not* be courteous landlords who let you know of changes in advance so you can prepare. Facebook is a great example. For years I knew a number of successful salespeople, particularly in the B2C area, who at no cost generated huge traffic on their Facebook business pages. They could reliably post articles, pictures, or other snippets of information, and within a few minutes of blasting it out, they would begin getting "likes" and comments. These would soon translate into leads and sales. It was a wonderful world for these salespeople, as they were able to consistently get sales by simply repeating the process over and over again.

Then, without any notice, Facebook's rules changed and the number of people who would receive updates dramatically reduced. It didn't take long for pain to set in, and companies realized if they wanted more visibility on Facebook, they would need to pay for advertising. Did we not recognize that Facebook would be expected to grow its revenue when it became a publicly traded company? Facebook changed the rules, and because we were playing at their tables, we would now have to ante up—and ante up big.

A huge factor we can never forget is what a social media site allows us to do today may not be there tomorrow, regardless of what we might think or how loudly we stomp our feet when they change the rules. Am I saying social media sites are not where we should spend our time? No, social media sites can be a great prospecting tool. But where I deviate from most people is I believe social media sites are just *one* prospecting tool. They're not the *only* prospecting tool.

You may choose to not use social media sites to prospect, but that doesn't mean you should ignore them. The title of this book is *High-Profit Prospecting*, and my intention is to show you how to find better prospects who, in turn, will be better customers for you. If you want better customers, you need to be a better salesperson. That means being better than your competitor at using every avenue possible to increase confidence in the minds of prospects.

Social media sites (and for that matter, the entire Internet) allow us to create a digital trail that anyone can access 24/7. It is important to realize your profile and activity on social media sites is picked up by search engines, and for most people these sites will pop up the highest in an online search of your name. This is the easiest way for you to create more confidence with your customers and prospects, and even generate leads. A key premise we can't forget is the greater the level of confidence the customer has in us, the greater probability we have of closing a profitable sale.

Why Do You Think It's Called "Social"?

The biggest challenge with social media sites is they're too heavy on the "social," and as a result, they can wind up becoming a giant time suck. The amount of time people can spend on them makes me sick. Social media sites are nothing more than a virtual 24/7 networking event. Have you attended networking events in your community put on by a local organization or business group? In the early days of my consulting business, I attended quite a few, thinking they would be a great way to develop local business. Wrong! What I quickly found was the crowds at these events always tended to include the same people. Not only were they the same people, but they also came from the same professions: insurance, financial planning, real estate, accounting, and banking.

The reason I relate social media with live networking events is because many times the audience winds up being similar from event to event. Repetition is certainly a good thing, as I see it as one of the key factors to a prospecting program's success. The problem is it takes too much time to create a big enough presence on social media sites to make a difference. Combine this with how long it can take prospects to see your value, and it becomes clear that too much investment in the process can become a misuse of your time.

I'm sure there are plenty of people who will disagree strongly with my views, but my big concern is time. The only asset that is limited in business is time, specifically *your* time. Spending hours a day on social media sites might give you a rush when seeing the number of likes, followers, and connections, but these have little value until you covert them into customers. One of the worst things we can believe is that all of our social media connections are leads waiting to be converted to prospects, and ultimately customers. I'm an optimist and I always want to see the upside, but let's get back to reality and accept the fact that a lot of our connections have zero potential.

Recently, I had a telephone conversation with a business owner who I know through work we both did several years ago with a trade association. The association changed management and chose to embrace social media one hundred percent as the way to grow membership and create additional revenue streams. I remember hearing about the group making the move when it first happened, and I thought to myself how the plan was most likely going to end poorly.

In my conversation with this business owner, he confirmed the notion I had. The association had burned through their reserves, all the while achieving none of the goals they had set forth to accomplish. If you were to have monitored their social media presence, you would have thought they were succeeding. They were putting out a lot of great content, and from all appearances, they were doing social media right. It might have had the appearance of being right, but it was wrong because they couldn't convert the awareness into revenue. You can't eat clicks and likes!

You Mean I Can't Spend All Day on Social Media?

Social media sites are like a giant suction machine. They can suck you in ever so slowly, and before you know it you've spent hours upon hours online. Argue with me all you want that what you're doing is prospecting or at least gathering leads, and I'll tell you that what you're doing is keeping yourself busy. But are you busy doing the right stuff? The question I like to ask salespeople is, "If you had zero income and you needed to close a sale quickly to put food on your table, in what activity would you invest your time?"

Yes, You Do Need a Strategy

Ask yourself, "Do I have a social media strategy?" The majority of salespeople do not have one, and I've found even those who do typically have nothing more than a vague plan at best. One of the worst things we can do is assume that how we use social media in our personal lives is how we should use it in our professional lives. Many people place too much emphasis on Facebook or Instagram and too little on LinkedIn, especially those in B2C.

Now comes a popular question: "Do I need to spend money to execute my social media plan?" The answer is both "yes" and "no." You don't need to spend anything to develop and execute a social media plan as one of your prospecting tools. The only thing I spend money on is buying a higher level of LinkedIn service that allows me to see for longer periods of time who has viewed my profile and to send out more messages. Even though I like these advantages, I can't say it's a game changer I can't live without. The reason I share this is because too many salespeople jump into buying every social media service and program they can. I find these programs are a lot like physical fitness equipment. A lot of people buy it, but few people actually use it.

Here's the argument for buying upgraded services and other programs: if you're looking to create awareness and scale significantly, then using programs and buying ad placement certainly is the right way to go. I am not, however, going to elaborate on specific products and services in this book because there are so many and they are constantly changing. Be cautious and do your research. I will, however, recommend Jay Baer at www.jaybaer.com/, because I think he does an excellent job reviewing and commenting upon different social media tools and statistics. His expertise is spot on and always current.

Failing to take the time to respond thoughtfully to the following questions about your social media strategy is only going to create more problems for you. It's easy to think because you know what other people have done to find success that all you need to do is copy them. That's insanity. As much as we want to think we can mirror what another person has done or is doing, the Internet is simply too brutal to allow two people to have the same results.

From my own experience, I can tell it is impossible to replicate someone else's plan. I know, because I've tried—not once, not twice, but multiple times, and each time the only thing that happened was I wasted too much time and resources. And other people have mirrored my successes, only to find failure. The Internet changes every day, and that's why whatever you do, it must be done with skepticism. Know the rules of the game could change at any time. Remember my comment at the start of this about building a home on land you don't own? Enough said. Let's look deeper at the questions.

Defining Your Social Media Strategy

Why do I want to use social media sites?

- Am I looking to generate leads or stay in touch with current customers?
- How much of my own time and effort is it going to take to build and monitor my own personal presence and profile?
- Does what I sell require the marketplace to become educated, or are people already familiar with what I sell?

What does my personal profile currently say about me on social media?

- Are there changes I need to make to how I currently use social media?
- Do I have connections and relationships on social media that could compromise my ability to use social media as a business tool?
- Do I own my name? Are there others on the Internet with the same name as me, and is what they're doing putting me at risk?

What is my company's policy regarding social media? What can I do?

- How firm are the policies, and is there someone I need to discuss this with?
- What are others in the company in my position doing with social media?

What resources are already available to me from my own website or my company's website that I can leverage?

- What items on my company's website can I use to my advantage on social media?
- Does my company have social media pages already that I should leverage?

What is the timeline I'm working under for building my presence on social media?

- How long am I willing to wait until I see a payout from my efforts? (Typically, whatever you feel is the time it will take, be prepared for it to take two or three times as long.)

What is my plan for getting leads and how will I respond to them?

- Will I respond to leads via the social media site, or will I attempt to connect with them via email or telephone?
- How will I enter responses into my CRM system to ensure proper follow-up?

What sites are my prospects and customers most likely using?

- (Limit the number of social media sites you are on. It's better to have a strong presence on one site than barely exist on three.)

How much effort is it going to take to create a strong enough presence on the site?

- Can I do this during my non-selling hours on weekends and evenings?
- Are there other activities I will need to remove from my calendar to have enough time to do social media right?

What are the tools I can use to help me automate my social media work?

- Where can I find the right tools, and what is it going to take to get them functioning properly?

Do I have a way to accurately measure the return on investment from my social media efforts?

- Am I segmenting leads effectively to know how I get them?
- Do I have a way to record in my CRM system leads I get through social media?

What legal parameters do I need to consider due to the profession or industry I'm in?

- Are there restrictions with how I set up my profile and what I can say?
- Are there restrictions about what I can do and with whom I can interact?

Is there a better use of my time?

- What other activities am I not spending enough time on now that with additional time could help me be more productive with prospecting?

How is social media used currently in my industry?

- Who uses it well and why do I think that? What's my proof?
- Is my industry ahead or behind the social media curve and why?

Do not rush answering these questions. The time you take answering them will pay out immensely by saving you time on social media.

It's a Slippery Slope

Answering the "how" and "when" can be a slippery slope. I remember far too well the first time this discussion came up. I was sitting in a breakout session in 2004 at the National Speakers Association annual conference, discussing social media and its role in business. The debate was lively! In the room were more than one hundred people focused on both B2B and B2C markets. People were shocked—and I'll put myself in that group—when other people said you needed to spend fifteen minutes a day on social media sites. To me, fifteen minutes was fourteen minutes too long. Fast-forward to today, and the going notion would be fifteen minutes is too little time. Many people might say something like a minimum of ninety minutes each day should be the norm, which to me is way too much! All this leads me to wonder what the norm will be in five years.

I'm not sharing this to say you need to spend more time on social media. No, I'm a huge proponent of spending as little time as possible on social media. By now you've come to sense that I do not see social media as being the perfect solution. It's *one* tool for prospecting; it is by no means the primary tool. Your time spent on social media must be time you would not spend on more productive prospecting activities!

Don't tell me how the time you spend on social media is the most effective way to prospect. I'm not buying it, and I'm pushing back. Yes, you can prospect on social media (I've devoted the next chapter exclusively to this topic), but I'm pushing back for two reasons. First, all social media sites are full of distractions that will pull you away from more productive work. Second, most social media activity is not in the moment. You're not posting things on social media and simultaneously having a discussion with a lead or prospect. Sure, there are exceptions, but by and large people do not live on social media sites waiting for you to connect with them.

The amount of time you spend on social media should start at one hour per week, and any increase beyond that should be earned. I'm serious about this—if you don't place firm limits, I guarantee you will suffer from what I like to call "social media creep." This is the tendency to spend just a few more minutes each day or each week on the sites, not realizing the bulk of time it's taking from your other activities.

I advocate breaking the hour into three twenty-minute segments each week: two on weeknights and the third sometime during the weekend. Breaking up your one hour over three occasions per week will give you more than enough time to post, comment, share, and connect. What it won't do is give you enough time to wander around watching stupid cat videos! Unless you're in the cat market, watching cat videos is not going to put food on your table.

Caution! What You Post Will Be Used Against You

Regarding what to post, the answer is, "Be wise!" It never ceases to amaze me how people will post photos with funny captions that also are quite insulting. Posting a comment or a picture of a city you happen to be in for a business trip and saying how boring it is might seem amusing to people in your hometown, but it's not going to win you any friends with customers or prospects in the city you're visiting. Don't believe you can keep your Facebook page or your Instagram account separate from business. Sorry, but that idea died with dial-up.

You can position your social media accounts to do different things. Let me break down for you how I use social media accounts. First, remember that my business is about helping companies and salespeople find and retain better customers to allow them to close more deals at higher prices. I do this primarily through my speaking and writing, along with training and consulting. My target audience is B2B companies and associations, and my buyers are mid-level and higher. As you can imagine, my number one social media site is LinkedIn. The other sites I use are Twitter and Facebook. Yes, I have accounts on YouTube, Pinterest, and Instagram, but I don't do a lot with them, simply because of the limited return on investment for my time.

If you're in B2C, your primary sites may very well be Facebook, Instagram, and Pinterest. A risk is stereotyping sites. Many view Pinterest as a site primarily for fashion, design, food, and crafts. Don't tell that to the *Harvard Business Review*; it has a huge presence on Pinterest. They use the site to develop new readers and reach people who are not familiar with their product.

It's impossible to lay out in a single book everything you should do on each social media site—let alone a single chapter. I'll show you what you can do on a few select sites to help you generate leads. In the next chapter, I'll discuss in more depth some social media prospecting strategies. A big note of caution: never allow social media sites to push updates and notifications to your email. The last thing you want is updates and alerts taking over your inbox, and let's be real, most of these messages are unnecessary.

LinkedIn

Build your personal profile, and a separate company profile page if you have your own company. The best way to build your profile is by following the model of other experts in your field. I have several peers whose profiles I look at every six months to make sure what I'm doing is fresh and relevant. I also take note of the groups they belong to. I'm not looking to copy verbatim what they do, but I use it as a way of judging the value of what I'm doing. (Go ahead and check out my LinkedIn profile at www.linkedin.com/in/markhunter/.)

Having as robust a profile as possible is essential, because most people don't realize LinkedIn is essentially a giant search engine. Have you ever wondered why certain people have viewed your profile? Chances are it's because your name came up in a LinkedIn search—or broader than that, a Google or Bing search. LinkedIn has established itself with enough credibility on the Internet that searches involving a person's name will many times return their LinkedIn profile page as one of the top search items.

Groups are a key part of your LinkedIn profile, and I believe in joining as many groups as possible. Some people say that doesn't make sense, and my argument is I need to have as big a web presence as possible. Join groups that meet the following criteria:

- ▶ Trade or industry groups where prospects are likely to be members
- ▶ Local business or trade groups
- ▶ Academic groups representing schools you attended or with which you have connections
- ▶ Peer groups consisting of people from whom you can learn

If you limit the connections you accept, you'll never be able to maximize LinkedIn to gain prospects. The key with LinkedIn (as with every other social media site) is to build awareness, and that means having as many people in your network as possible. The more people who are connected with you means the more people who will be able to see your full profile and your updates and ultimately provide you with more opportunities to generate leads. Kurt Shaver, LinkedIn sales expert and creator of the Social Selling Boot Camp, summed it up well when he noted, "LinkedIn, with all of its sharing capabilities, allows each salesperson to be a mini-marketer to attract prospects." (You can learn more from Kurt at www.thesalesfoundry.com/ and, of course, on LinkedIn at www.linkedin.com/in/kurtshaver/.)

Yes, there are some connections you should reject. Although each person needs to define their own criteria, the criteria I use is to decline any invitation that does not have a profile picture, has bad grammar in the title, or clearly is a person with less than honorable intentions. Go ahead and follow old school rules of connecting only with people you've met, and your competitors will thank you for making it that much easier for them. Your total time reviewing and accepting connections should be no more than five minutes per week.

Posting and commenting on content is critical. My view is to keep things simple. Personally, I repost on LinkedIn articles I write on my company website. Additionally, I will push to LinkedIn a key article I might have seen on a news site that I believe those who follow me will find of value. Total time to do this is maybe ten minutes per week. Posting content is critical because it allows others to get to know you and what you're thinking. You may not have company blog posts you can push to LinkedIn, but you can send several key news articles each week.

The majority of my LinkedIn time each week is responding to people who comment on things I've posted or making quick comments on other things I feel are worthy. This activity takes at most twenty minutes per week. Thanking people and making comments builds community and, as I'll explain more in the next chapter, it has helped me generate significant business opportunities.

Facebook

The approach I take with LinkedIn is the same approach I use with my Facebook homepage and my business page. The same rules also apply to connections, although I'm a little tighter on my personal page, where I will occasionally post pictures of my family. Due to the number of business connections I have on Facebook, I also will post business content. Connecting with business associates, including customers, on Facebook is an excellent way to stay in touch and for you to know what is going on in their lives. No, this isn't creepy. I'm not forcing a connection on anyone, but what I've found is connecting with business associates and customers has allowed us to know each other better, which has in turn strengthened our business relationships.

I spend a total of five minutes on Facebook each week for business. Notice I say each week "for business," because I consider the majority of my other time on Facebook as personal time, which is away from business.

Twitter

Twitter is the social media site that confuses most people. Unless you're in an industry that places value on Twitter or are in a group of people that use it, I think it is wise to tread cautiously. Because it has a high volume of short, instantaneous posts, it can really pull you in—and before long, you have wasted an hour of selling time.

Tech, startups, and many consumer companies use Twitter extensively, but I know many other industries where Twitter is not relevant. As aggressively as some sectors use it, other sectors ignore it. This is why I can't stand it when people proclaim how powerful it is as a business tool. It *is* powerful if you play in an industry where it is used. I've gained several nice pieces of business from Twitter, but it has all been in either the tech sector or a startup. As with other sites, the key to Twitter is building your profile to represent yourself in the best way possible. One of the best ways to do this is by seeing what your peers are doing.

Do not get sucked into the Twitter time machine. Check it twice a week. Using a tool such as Hootsuite, you can load one or two original Tweets, find a couple of Tweets you like and re-Tweet them, and be done with it until the next week. An easy way to find Tweets you can re-Tweet is to follow five people who you think are really smart and who Tweet good stuff. Take a minute to look at their Twitter streams, and you'll easily find a couple of Tweets you like and can share.

Yes, you can go much deeper with how you leverage Twitter, but the word of caution I give is to make sure each minute of time you devote to Twitter is a minute that would not be better spent doing something else.

The Circus Continues

There are other social media sites I could list and discuss, but you get the point. It's a circus trying to keep up. Don't do anything unless it fits your target market and you can get a payback for your efforts—and that payback for your efforts can't be in five or ten years. If you don't start seeing results within six months, then you need to start modifying your plan. If after a year you're still not seeing anything, then it's time to take a deep breath and reexamine your strategy. Don't completely ditch everything (as the Internet does continue to evolve, and what doesn't work one month might work the next), but rethink where you allocate your resources. Finally, I put this just ahead of the chapter on how to prospect using social media for one simple reason. If you expect to be able to use social media to find prospects, you first have to have a platform from which to do it.

CHAPTER 18

Prospecting via Social Media

When doing research for this book and talking with sales-people about problem areas, many questioned me on how to prospect using social media. Salespeople from both large and small companies were quick to describe the various attempts they had made on social media without much success. Many shared stories about buying programs from so-called "social media experts," only to find they were not helpful at all. Sales managers also were quick to share their frustrations with marketing departments taking money from the sales budgets and spending it to push content and buy clicks as a way to generate leads from social media sites.

The "Experts" Aren't Experts

With all the confusion, I feel it's time to get deep into the mud and call out all the "experts" who claim that by using their methods, you too can be successful prospecting on the Internet. The number of courses out there claiming to know the inside secrets to prospecting with LinkedIn, Facebook, and other sites will make any head spin. I struggle with these "experts" and here's why: they all claim that by using their methodologies you will find success. But what they're selling is a dream. With enough false hype (and oh, by the way, cold emails), you too could be successful selling a dream. But wait, there's more, as they would say. For us, we're selling a real product or a real service that creates a tangible benefit or outcome for the customer.

Let's cut to the chase. Social media can work as a prospecting tool. It will allow you to connect with many people you would never be able to reach via email or the telephone. Social media is changing the way we prospect in the same way the telephone changed the way salespeople prospected when it arrived on the scene. The Internet and social media sites are also changing advertising—much in the same way television did when it came of age in the 1950s and 1960s. When you begin to accept the Internet as just another transition in how you connect with customers, you can finally begin to use it effectively.

It wouldn't be fair for me to say that what I'm going to share will work perfectly for you. If I were to make that claim, I would be no different than the "experts" I just ranted about. But don't think with this disclaimer that what I'm sharing isn't relevant. It is! The strategy I'm about to share will bring you results; the only question is what level of results. The amount of business I've received over the years from social media prospecting is significant, and there is no way I would have secured the business without social media. My success alone should discount anyone thinking social media does not deliver additional business.

Before even thinking about using social media to prospect, you first should make sure you're practicing the techniques I laid out in the previous chapter. It all comes down to a simple fact: the bigger a footprint you have on social media sites, the more opportunities you'll have to prospect. Not only will you have more prospecting options, but you also will provide prospects with more social proof of your credibility. Everyone you prospect via social media is going to check your profile before dialoguing with you. High-profit prospecting is about creating a high level of confidence about you in your prospects, and a key part of the overall strategy can be your social media footprint.

Your Time Is Not Their Time

In the previous chapter, I said to limit your time to one hour per week on social media sites. If you do choose to use social media sites as a prospecting tool, you will need to devote more time to these sites. My guideline is to still spend one hour per week maintaining social media, and your other time on social media is part of your lower-value prospecting time. I say lower-value because it shouldn't be during your best hours of the day when you should be on the phone. I recommend you set aside a block of time to prospect and develop leads via email and social media.

It's important to never lose sight of the fact that people will not necessarily respond in a timely manner. It's easy for us in sales to think that because we're on social media sites such as LinkedIn, everyone is. The majority of people who are active on LinkedIn fall into one of three broad categories: salespeople, HR, or people in employment transition. Mid-level managers and others with whom you're attempting to connect may check social media sites only once a week or once a month. If your target is the C-suite, most likely you're not going to find them on social media at all. This doesn't mean social media sites can't get into the C-suite; it just means you might need to use a path by way of a mid-level manager to whom you are connected. Facebook, Twitter, Instagram, Pinterest, and other social media sites all have different target audiences. Regardless of their focus and your attitude toward them, don't expect your prospect to have the same attitude toward these sites.

In my work with clients, I have them look at how they prospect with social media using three different approaches:

1. Dialogue directly to create a lead or prospect. This by far is the most efficient way to prospect, as you're reaching out to build dialogue with the person you've identified as a potential prospect.
2. Prospect with people who can connect you with the prospects you are trying to reach. For many salespeople, this is the only way to use social media if the prospects you want to reach are not on social media. With this approach, you're reaching out and dialoguing with people who can connect you with the prospects.
3. Respond to people inquiring about you. This is where a bigger footprint has the potential to create more opportunities. I've had major opportunities come to me simply from people sending me messages via LinkedIn and Twitter.

The first and second approaches use the same strategies, but with the second one it can take much longer to get to the prospect because you need to go through someone else.

Why more salespeople don't use social media to prospect is amazing to me. I can only speculate, but I wonder if people are turned off to this approach because of the numerous bad prospecting messages they've received from others via social media. Just because others don't do it right is not a reason for you to not do it. You just need to know the correct way.

Taking the First Step

Finding potential leads begins with monitoring who views your profile. I pay close attention to who is checking my profile, and if I see any potential leads, I immediately reach out. Some might say this borders on stalking, but I keep coming back to what I wrote earlier in this book: if you believe what you do can help others, then you owe it to them to connect. How I reach out will vary based on what the social media site allows me to do. My preferred way is to ask for a connection and message them within the site's structure to engage them in a conversation. Remember, the person looking at your profile did so because they saw something of interest. It's your job now to follow up.

If you do have access to view the prospect's full profile, it is extremely important you take note of everything. You're looking for topics you might have in common with them, such as personal or professional connections and interest groups. In the preceding chapter, I shared the importance of being part of groups to which your prospects most likely belong. You often can find these by looking at their profiles.

It is best to keep what I refer to as direct prospecting via social media "social" in nature at the early stage. I will rarely send a note to someone via social media with a direct request to uncover an immediate business need. The most common approach I use in the initial message is to ask a question or make a comment about something the two of us have in common. It's now up to the receiver to make the next move, and with social media we have to be patient that the next move may not occur for several weeks. The way the person responds will determine the next step. Typically, I will keep my response focused solely on responding to what they sent to me in their response.

After a second response, I will then move forward and begin to shift the discussion to a topic that allows me to uncover a need I can fulfill. As soon as the conversation moves in this direction, I also look to move it "offline" from the social media site. To me this is an easy way to begin qualifying the contact and seeing if they could be a prospect. Someone who is willing to move the discussion to email or the telephone certainly expresses some interest. Someone who does not want to move away from the social media site may still be a viable lead, but it may take more time to be certain.

If you're in B2C, you can easily become overwhelmed with people who want to dialogue forever on a social media site for no other reason than they enjoy it. The problem is that their enjoyment is taking up your time. If they're not willing to move "offline," I've found you can take this as a strong signal that what you have is not a prospect, but merely a time-waster.

Recently, I was working with a sales force that sold software systems in the enterprise space. Their prospects typically were either in IT or finance. The plan we discussed centered first on using traditional prospecting methods, such as telephone and email, to reach them. If the prospect failed to respond to traditional methods, then the plan would be to reach them via social media.

In sharing this strategy with the sales team, several of them immediately asked if it would be appropriate to reach prospects via social media if they had rejected their overtures via traditional methods. My response was by all means yes—the initial contact is social in nature, so it is certainly appropriate. Needless to say, I was appalled the salespeople asked the question in the first place. If I believe I can help others, don't I owe it to them to connect? There is absolutely no reason why salespeople should not use social media to prospect.

For this sales team, because they operate in the B2B arena, the optimal social media platform to use is LinkedIn. If you're in B2C, it will most likely be Facebook, Instagram, Twitter, or Pinterest. The main problem with using social media to prospect is the lack of a direct connection with the person you're trying to reach. For the sake of saving time, this is the primary reason I suggest upgrading your level of service with

LinkedIn to allow you to reach more people. When using this approach, the first message I send is through LinkedIn. There, I will follow similar guidelines to how I use email. If you know some personal information about the person, build your message around that information.

This might sound trivial, but be sure you record in your CRM system any prospecting activity you do via social media. On more than a few occasions, I've seen salespeople lose all credibility when they finally do dialogue with a prospect, but fail to remember what they said or did weeks or months earlier when reaching out to that prospect on social media. This is just one more reason why I highly recommend using a CRM system that allows you to integrate your social media activity. The time you save will pay for itself many times over.

Search, Seek, Connect

Groups and group postings are another way to uncover potential leads. Depending on the social media site you're using and its parameters, sending messages to group members can pay off. Unlike targeting specific people, create more general postings to fit a broader profile of prospects when you reach out to a group.

I strongly suggest contacting group members on a weekend or in the evening when the time could not be spent on a more productive sales activity. Uncovering prospects via social media groups can be time consuming, and I advise salespeople to do it only if they can control themselves from spending too much time on social media sites. This approach has as much potential to B2C salespeople as it does to B2B salespeople. If someone who received the group message responds, I recommend using the same approach as with direct prospects: reply back with another comment or question that builds on the first. The second response you receive from them can then be your guide to knowing if they're worth pursuing.

A high-return activity when identifying potential leads is doing keyword searches of job titles or company names. Never underestimate the search engine capabilities of a social media site to help uncover new opportunities. Your ability to connect with any leads you identify will be driven by the parameters set by the social media site, but typically there is some method you can use to contact them. As with the other social media strategies, the approach I use and recommend to sales teams is to make the initial message a question or a comment about something they will find of value. Because it's social media, a response could come in five minutes or five weeks. Do not take the speed of the response as an indication of their interest. Response time is more often driven by how often they look at the social media site and/or the settings they have created to receive messages.

The Fallacy of the Numbers

My goal is to have you as a connection on social media. Let's be honest, there's not a person out there who has not been mesmerized at one time or another with the idea of building their list of connections. Just remember, you can't eat connections. Having connections is meaningless from a sales aspect until they turn into profitable business.

As I discussed in the previous chapter, I encourage you to connect with those people who want to connect with you and fit your criteria for acceptance. When people connect with me, I'm going to look at their profiles; if they have merit, I will reach out to them immediately. Be cautious, however, with the time you spend. There's a reason it's called "social media." There are a lot of people who like to be just that—social. Conversations are great, but they can take up time, which is your most precious resource.

The objective of the connection is to begin developing confidence, which may allow you to later get connected with someone else. Your connections will create other connections from similar circles, which can create still more connections, not to mention more confidence. Your connections have the ability to see what you post, which in turn increases their awareness and—yes, I will say it again—their confidence in you. On more than one occasion, I've had people reach out to me based on a recommendation from another person with whom I was connected on social media. This approach is extremely important if you're targeting senior-level people or the C-suite. These people tend not to be on social media sites, but it is not unusual for people one level below them to be on the sites. When you connect with people at this level, you have opportunities to build their confidence in you, which may compel them to think connecting you with senior-level people is a good idea.

The further up you go in any organization, the more critical it is for you to have a trail of supporters who feel confident in you and know you have strategic value to their company. When people trust your competence, they will be far more willing to make a connection on your behalf.

You Mean to Tell Me I Won't Have Instant Customers?

We'd all like to think we could turn a social media presence into a continuous source of new leads and instant customers, simply from people commenting on what we share. The odds of that happening are simply not anywhere close to being in your favor, despite what the "Internet experts" might want you to believe.

The best approach for finding success is to carry out the strategy I outlined in the previous chapter for posting updates. Your objective with your posts is to increase your level of stature and build the confidence people have in you. Closely monitor those who view and share your posts. The people who share, as well as the people with whom they share updates, may be leads worthy of your follow up. There will also be people who post comments, and they also may be leads worthy of a follow up. Your follow-up comments to these people should merely build on the original posts.

Developing ongoing conversations with people certainly can be beneficial, but it also can take up too much of your valuable time. My rule is to exchange comments with people on a limited basis if and when I find the comments insightful. The challenge is not becoming so engrossed in online conversations that they quickly take your time away from other activities. It can go both ways, though, because you do become known by what you post and the circles you run in, and that alone can create leads and ultimately business. I'll share two examples. The first is a person I traded comments with off and on for over a year. Without me asking, this person connected me with someone else, and that person eventually became one of my customers. The second example is a person who reached out to me and said they were doing so only because they had been following me on social media for years and liked the comments I shared. Was this incremental business I wasn't expecting? It sure was; however, I will freely argue I'm not sure it was worth the investment of time. I say this because I don't know for sure how much time went into getting those pieces of business—and that is why I say social media can occupy far more of your time than you even realize.

Social Media Sites Are Merely Search Engines

Social media is here to stay, and while we don't know what it's going to look like tomorrow, we must figure out how to best leverage it today. Recently, I was having a discussion with a salesperson who is clearly at the top of her industry. Few people can do what she does, and she has the track record to show for it. Her market is B2B, and she sells a service with a typical sales cycle between two and five months. I've had many discussions with her about the value of social media, in particular LinkedIn. She believes social media sites try to do everything possible to make it difficult for salespeople to use them. In her mind, a perfect social media site would be one that gives her complete accurate information and a way to message contacts via the site, as well as directly.

She doesn't use social media sites to message prospects using the approaches I've presented in this chapter, but she still uses the sites daily as a search and verification tool. The reason she doesn't use social media sites for messaging is because she believes people don't respond quickly enough. However, if you ask her if she looks at a prospect's profile on LinkedIn before calling them, she'll say, "Of course I do!" Ask her if she sends out a request to connect with a prospect on LinkedIn after she's talked with them on the phone, and she'll say, "Of course I do!" Ask her if she sends a connection request to other people in the same company where she is prospecting, and she'll say, "Of course I do!" And ask her if she uses LinkedIn to gain contact information or titles she can use when she makes a phone call, and she'll say, "Of course I do!"

This high-performing salesperson uses LinkedIn not as a tool to send and receive messages, but as a tool to aid her in her other prospecting efforts. You may be like her and choose not to use most of the strategies

I've shared in this chapter. That's fine, but I will say failing to use social media in at least some capacity to prospect will put you at a serious disadvantage.

Going back to the early days of the telephone, I'm sure there were companies that failed to embrace it, believing there was no way anyone would want to do business with someone they couldn't see. I'm sure there were companies in the early days of television that saw it as nothing but a fad, void of any genuine opportunity to effectively advertise. I'm wondering how things worked out for these companies. I suspect they did just fine for a while, but over the long term, the telephone and television were changes you couldn't ignore. We can say the same today with social media and the impact it has on prospecting. You can ignore it and be fine for a while, but don't come back to me in a few years and complain about your lack of customers.

PART IV:

THE TOUGH STUFF

CHAPTER 19

Getting Past the Gatekeeper

For me, college was built around "outside activities" that frequently had me in conversation with the dean of students. My interaction with the dean was never on my terms. The two of us didn't quite see eye to eye on a few details, such as campus rules. When I would be "asked" to meet with the dean, I would arrive at the scheduled time at his office, where I faced the "gatekeeper" (the dean's assistant). She knew her role and played the part extremely well, as her job was to make sure everyone knew she and her boss ran the campus. Over time and through my visits with the dean, the assistant and I began to at least achieve a mutual understanding for each other, even if we weren't exactly becoming best friends. What began as me being a scared underclassman arriving to face the tyranny of the dean over time turned into me arriving as an upperclassman asking the assistant about her weekend. I even would ask her about her summer plans and, more importantly, how she felt the dean would handle the impending conversation with me. I look back at it all and wonder why I didn't receive class credit for either sales prospecting or crisis management!

Gatekeepers have a variety of job roles, from the lifelong receptionist who answers every phone call, to the executive assistant who has key company insights, to the mid-level assistant who may work for several vice presidents. Regardless of who they are or the roles they play, nearly all of them are professional and are masters of performing their jobs to the letter. Our job is to never demean them, but rather see them as the key assets they are—to their bosses and to us.

Naturally, the first move when you reach a gatekeeper is to ask if the person you're trying to reach is available. Don't blow smoke if the gatekeeper asks something like, "Who may I say is calling and what is this in reference to?" Be up front and state your name and company. The key is how you respond to the second half of the question regarding "why" you are calling. You want to state what you believe will be a benefit or positive outcome for the person you're trying to reach.

Here are a few examples. As with the scripts in the earlier chapters, I provide these to give you ideas. Base the specific wording you use on the particular outcome or benefit you provide:

> We help companies minimize labor.
>
> We allow companies to gain more output from their
> data centers.
>
> We help people achieve the financial resources they need.
>
> We help improve safety.
>
> We help cut capital expenditures.

It is important you do not get any more specific than necessary, because you want the gatekeeper to come back and ask you a question. When the gatekeeper engages you, it allows you to now begin gaining insights from this valuable source. Their job is to discern if they can trust you enough to forward you to the person you are trying to reach. They need to determine whether or not you will embarrass them.

Use the gatekeeper to your advantage by asking them questions. One way to do this is by asking them the same questions you would ask the decision maker. Many times the gatekeeper will realize they can't answer the questions and will then connect you with the person and/or department who can. As you ask questions, be certain you don't use a condescending tone of voice. One approach is to begin by saying, "May I ask you a few questions?" I've used this approach on numerous occasions and have found it to be extremely effective, especially if you talk with this gatekeeper more than once in your attempts to reach the decision maker.

Always Treat Them with Respect

On every call, let your personality come through and allow the gate-keeper to see you as a normal person who is merely doing your job, just like them. In the end, it's just people dealing with people, and I'm always amazed at how smoothly a conversation can go when there is mutual respect. Every gatekeeper has their standard way of handling calls, and yet there's not one gatekeeper who won't make an exception based on how they're treated. Too many times, a gatekeeper who is tasked with answering the telephone all day can begin to feel like a lower-level employee. When you treat them well and allow them to see you as a person they can trust, you'll be astounded at the amount of information they will share. This is especially important if you turn the lead or prospect into a customer and contact the company on a regular basis.

Persistence *can* and *will* pay off. Remember if it's hard for you to get in, then it's also hard for your competition. But most likely, they're not as persistent as you. Don't take rejection from a gatekeeper person-ally. If you allow a rejection by a gatekeeper to negatively impact you, there is little chance you will ever be successful. If the same gatekeeper responds each time you call, then you need to make sure you have a new reason for the call. This is one reason I'm a big proponent of having new and relevant information every time you make a call.

While You Look Left, I'll Go Right

You can never forget that what you sell, whether a product or service, is going to benefit the prospect with whom you're trying to connect. As much as it may benefit the prospect and others, there can and will be times when the gatekeeper simply won't understand or care. They will not allow you to get past them. But just because you can't get through one door doesn't mean the location is closed. No, it merely means it's time to use another door.

Other approaches you can try:

1. Most gatekeepers work traditional hours, so calling either before eight in the morning or after five or during lunch may

result in someone else answering the phone. The person who is merely filling in might just be more accommodating in connecting people or sharing information.

2. Call and ask for the accounts receivable department. Every company is eager to collect money. By asking for that department, you'll be connected—and believe me when I say this department definitely will answer the phone. When you are connected, be up front and state whom you are trying to reach.

3. Call one or two digits off from the phone number you've been calling. When the person answers, be straightforward and say the name of the person you're trying to reach. This is not a dark technique. No, it's totally valid, because you're telling the person who answers right up front whom you're trying to reach. Use this approach once you've exhausted all attempts to connect via the direct number.

4. Call a different division or location, if the company has one. Use the other location as a way to learn the name of the person you should try to reach at the main location. If what you sell has a long sales cycle with multiple decision makers, reaching out to other divisions or locations can be extremely beneficial.

CHAPTER 20

Winning at the Enterprise Level

The common thread linking global giants with the smallest of companies is they're all comprised of people just like you and me. The only thing different is the number of zeros in their yearly results and the set of rules by which they play. Everything you've read so far in this book will help you get into even the largest of companies.

When prospecting big companies, your objective is to find out as rapidly as possible answers to these five questions:

1. What are the goals/objectives they need to accomplish?
2. What barriers are they facing?
3. What is the timeline they operate under?
4. Where is the power within the company?
5. What is the company's tolerance for risk?

That's it. There's no need to overcomplicate things. The challenge becomes finding the people who can help you uncover the answers to these questions, because only when you have answers will you know how you can assist each company.

Your objective is to avoid being routed to purchasing. If all you're looking for is a lead, then go ahead and go directly to purchasing, but the task of then converting the lead to a good prospect and ultimately to a customer will be difficult. Your best approach is to find people in the organization who will answer your questions and fill one of the critical roles in the customer buying process.

The Roles People Play

Ultimately, the lead you uncover also will help you find the seven types of people many salespeople encounter when selling to large companies:

1. *User:* The person who will use what you sell.
2. *Owner:* The person who owns the budget that will provide the funds to purchase.
3. *Decision Maker:* The person who owns the decision-making process.
4. *Champion:* The person who works on your behalf to advance the process.
5. *Influencer:* The person who wants to be involved in the decision-making process.
6. *Optimizer:* The person who is proactive in finding ways to create a better outcome.
7. *Road Blocker:* The person who, usually for their own gain, will attempt to sabotage or block a decision.

These seven people will not exist in every situation; however, the larger the company or the larger the project, the greater the number of people who will be looking to play a role in the decision. Your goal is to understand what position your lead is in and, as opportunities arise, to find other contacts in the company who will fill the other roles.

To connect, use the strategies I've discussed in previous chapters. But as you move forward to make contact, don't be lulled into a false sense of belief due to a person's title. The set of rules by which a big company plays starts with titles. I was working with one of the largest corporations in the world recently, and the person to whom I was talking had the title of "Commercial Services." On the surface this doesn't sound impressive, yet she was responsible for more than $1 billion in business! It would have been easy for me to assume she wouldn't have buying authority, but clearly that was not the case. A simple concept I go by is the bigger the company, the smaller the titles. The solution is in the questions you ask, because unless you have direct knowledge of the company's organizational structure you will never know going in who the various players are and, more importantly, what they actually do. To help uncover some of the mysteries within a company when it comes to titles, I use three different websites: LinkedIn, Data.com Connect, and Glassdoor. These three sites provide excellent insights into titles, and by reading job descriptions you will gain an overview as to a contact's span of control.

When making contact, never hide the fact that your goal is to get them as a customer. This does not mean you start the first contact by saying, "Buy from me now." No, you lead by trying to gain information to help you get answers to one or more of the five questions listed at the beginning of this chapter.

You may be with a small company looking to sell to the global corporation, but during your prospecting phase, you cannot allow the prospect to view you as a small company. The more they see you as a peer who speaks their language, understands their rulebook, and is not in awe of their company size, the greater your probability for success. People in large companies don't have time to train a salesperson on the nuances of how a big company works.

Best Practices

When I'm working with sales teams to develop their prospecting skills while dealing with large companies, I outline the following five best practice techniques:

1. At the end of any conversation, ask if there is somebody else in the company who also can give you input. Your objective is to expand your influence in the company as much as possible.
2. Try to find out how they have made similar buying decisions in the past, including budgeting issues, timelines, contract requirements, vendor approvals, and bidding processes. The earlier you know this information, the better you will understand the desired timeline and with whom you need to be working.

3. With each lead you get, regardless of the number of leads you have within a company, keep them engaged via email. Send them emails containing key information about the industry, a competitor, or other relevant insights. Your objective is to engage them enough to see you as a valued resource with great information.

4. Follow up with each person who appears in an email as a "cc." The same applies to anyone mentioned in a meeting or in a document. Your objective is to open as many connections as possible.

5. If someone says you should contact the purchasing department, your immediate response must be that now is not the time for you to contact purchasing, because there are too many questions you need answered.

These five steps will allow you to better understand who is filling each of the seven roles listed earlier in this chapter as you move through the selling process.

Finally, never allow a single lead to give you the impression they are your contact for the entire company. The larger the company, the more segmented it tends to be—meaning your lead may have influence over only a small part of the company. This is the key reason I believe you must always be prospecting big companies, regardless of the number of leads you may already have.

CHAPTER **21**

Is It Worth It to Even Try to Reach the C-suite?

Y ou want to connect with the C-suite. In fact, it's one of the biggest reasons you bought this book and have spent time reading each chapter. You've finally come to this one, dedicated solely to the C-suite. Without holding back any longer, let me give you the best advice I can. What works for every other type of prospect is not going to work with the C-suite. It's not that you should ignore all of the other chapters in this book—with a little bit of tweaking, those strategies will be effective with the C-suite and other top-level people. You simply must adjust how you use the techniques to fit the C-level.

John Spence, who has been working with CEOs for the past twenty years, and is recognized as one of the "Top 100 Business Leaders in America," confirms my belief that C-suite executives don't want to meet with salespeople, but they will meet with recognized industry experts who have a solid track record of delivering world-class solutions. John has a great quote I've heard him use many times when we've had the privilege of working together: "Be so good they can't ignore you." Well-stated indeed! (Check out John Spence at www.johnspence.com/.)

Before we get into the adjustments, it's important to validate if there is even a need to prospect the C-suite. If what you're selling is a consumable and does not require special budget considerations, then I'll challenge the need to even contact the C-suite. We've all been told the importance of creating relationships at the top and selling as high up in an organization as possible. It generally makes sense, but there are times

169 ▲

when *making sense* won't make you any money and may even wind up wasting your time.

Criteria for Prospecting the C-suite

Ask yourself, "Does what I sell . . .

- ▶ . . . require special budget considerations?
- ▶ . . . have strategic value to the customer?
- ▶ . . . have implications with regard to staffing needs?
- ▶ . . . allow the C-suite to achieve an annual objective that is currently at risk?
- ▶ . . . have significant implications on the long-term goals and objectives the CEO has set?

If what you are selling doesn't fit into one of the above scenarios, then spending time prospecting the C-suite or other senior-level people in a large company most likely will not generate a return versus your time invested. If, on the other hand, what you sell lines up with two or more of the above criteria, then you should prospect the C-suite.

Once you've decided to prospect the C-suite, it does not preclude you from reaching out to other people in the company. In fact, you generally must reach out to other people, but the purpose will be different. Your objective now is gaining insight and information to assist you in your meetings in the C-suite. The amount of time you spend on a particular company should only be in relationship to the value you expect to get should they become a customer.

They Think Differently Than the Average Prospect

If you've determined prospecting the C-suite makes sense and is worth your time, you need to identify what changes to make to your prospecting plan. To do this, explore what makes top-level people different than the average prospects.

C-suite and senior-level people are more likely to . . .

- ▶ . . . think in a longer time frame.
- ▶ . . . be less price-oriented.
- ▶ . . . think strategically.
- ▶ . . . be confident and focused.
- ▶ . . . be cautious with their comments.
- ▶ . . . think big.
- ▶ . . . understand the value and need for risk.
- ▶ . . . protect and value their time.
- ▶ . . . have high regard for integrity.
- ▶ . . . have a desire to learn.
- ▶ . . . be curious.
- ▶ . . . not want to be embarrassed.
- ▶ . . . protect their images.
- ▶ . . . be respectful of others.
- ▶ . . . place high value in people they trust.

This list is based on my work with more than one-thousand executives and senior-level people across countless companies and associations in the last twenty years. There will certainly be variances with each individual, but in twenty years I have not found one executive who does not embrace the majority of the items listed. The list is important with regard to prospecting, because it can guide you in understanding what it will take to successfully prospect senior-level people. Failing to understand the difference between lower-level prospects and senior-level prospects is why too many salespeople, upon making contact with the C-suite, are immediately transferred to the purchasing department. Members of the C-suite simply think differently, and that's often why they're in the C-suite. If you fail to take this into account when you prospect, you deserve to be pushed to the purchasing department—and *that* maybe is even generous.

The biggest change you need to make when prospecting the C-suite is altering your expectations regarding the time it will take to see results. When I'm reaching out to a CEO or another senior-level person, I look at time in terms of months and quarters, not days and weeks. If you want to eliminate any chance of reaching the C-suite, go ahead and pepper them with emails and phone calls every other day or even every week. With CEOs, contacting them more than once a month can begin to border on excessive.

They Play With a Different Rulebook

When building your C-suite prospecting strategy, you need to think about three things: confidence, trust, and referral. C-suite executives value their time, and before agreeing to meet with anyone, they want to ensure their time will not be wasted. Therefore, the people who get time on their calendars are either going to be people they already know or referrals from people they already trust. The referrals might only come from their assistants, but they are still referrals, because the assistants would not allow you access to the C-suite execs unless they first had trust and confidence in you.

A referral may also come from another person in the company who passes your name to the assistant. A few years ago, I received a phone call from an administrative assistant I had never met. The assistant was reaching out to inquire about having me speak to their entire company. We had a brief conversation, and the call resulted in me being invited to have a conversation with the president of the company. The outcome was not just a one-time speaking engagement, but a long-term relationship that was profitable for everyone. The reason it all came together was the assistant called me based on a relationship I had developed with a mid-level manager, who the president's assistant highly respected. The trust and confidence I was able to develop with the mid-level manager is what carried me to the C-suite. The mid-level manager lacked the buying authority to hire me, but he could refer me to those who could. Granted, you can't replicate this example at every company, but you will see it happen with some of your prospects. It worked for me, because the person with whom I initially developed the relationship was respected by the C-suite.

A fundamental rule I have when it comes to prospecting the C-suite is to never start more than one level below the C-suite. A key reason you don't want to start lower in an organization is not just the waste of time, but also because it can set you up for being banned forever from the C-suite. Remember, one of the traits listed that makes C-suite people different is how they protect their time. If the C-suite person knows you're already working with someone else in their company, they will be less likely to make time for you. Why should they, if they feel someone else can take care of your issue? If you want to be seen as valuable by the C-suite and worthy of their time, you not only must meet the criteria listed earlier in this chapter, but you also must have critical information that interests them.

Emailing the C-suite

Remember, the chances are not very good that the member of the C-suite you're targeting is going to see whatever you send. The exception is if you use the weekend email strategies described in chapter 15. An email for a C-suite person should follow a different format than what you would use in normal prospecting. First, do not discount the value of the assistant. Yes, the assistant position is going away in more and more companies; but in other companies the position still exists, merely with a different title.

If you have the contact information for the assistant or the person who serves that function, contact them directly. It is far more likely that an assistant will first read your email than the C-suite member. This does not mean the content should be different. The most important thing to remember when dealing with an assistant is you must treat them the same as you would the C-suite person. The assistant is vetting you and what you have to say, and he or she must have a level of confidence and trust in you if you want to have any opportunity for that person to refer you to the senior-level person.

The most effective email style for the C-suite is one that adheres to all of the normal prospecting guidelines. First and foremost, make sure you don't include any attachments and graphics. CEOs and others in the C-suite are skeptical of accepting anything that might contain a virus of any sort. Numerous CEOs have told me they will not under any circumstances open a file or click a link sent to them from anyone outside of their own companies. This only serves as another reminder of the role trust plays with people in senior-level positions.

Where the email rules change when targeting the C-suite is in the content and the format of the email. The format I have found to be the most effective is the "three-point/explanation" style: start your email with three bullet points, followed by two or three sentences explaining each bullet point. The power of this format is that it's concise. If the person receiving it only has time to view part of it, they at least see the bullet points.

Numerous salespeople have told me one of the key reasons they were ultimately able to meet with the C-suite members after using this format is because of their succinct communication styles.

Here is an example of an email used to reach a CEO:

To: Ross Jones

Subject: Fed Rate Impact on Q2

With the recent announcement on rates, several things appear to be at risk:

- Value of the dollar will impact Asian imports
- Capex spending will change for many companies
- Annual earnings

With the dollar continuing to gain value versus Asian currencies, we will see Asian competitors becoming more aggressive in how they price.

With the cost of borrowing money increasing, there is going to be pressure on many companies, which could result in them moving major purchases back a year.

All of the news coming out of the Fed implies there could be softness in the economy, which most likely means many firms could see their annual earnings at risk.

We have new findings from our global work and would be happy to share them with you and, more importantly, how you can protect your company and leverage these factors.

Looking forward to hearing from you and setting a time to meet. You can reach me at the number below.

Mark Hunter
The Sales Hunter
402-445-2110

Notice how the email is longer than a normal prospecting email and has a totally different flow. All of this is intentional, as it allows the person receiving it to read as little or as much as they want. If you have both the email addresses for the assistant and C-suite person, send it to both at the same time, listing the assistant in the "cc" field.

The right frequency for using this format is once a month. Once a month allows you to balance both respect for their time and the need for you to communicate valuable information.

Calling the C-suite

Due to the amount of information available on the Internet, getting the phone number for the CEO or another C-suite member often is not difficult—especially for publicly traded companies. When calling a senior-level person, the same rules apply as if you were calling anyone else. The call can go one of three ways: voicemail, another person answers, or the person you're trying to reach answers. Yes, this means being prepared for each scenario is essential.

Calling a senior-level person does require more sensitivity to ensure the other person doesn't view you as selling something. Senior-level people don't *buy* anything; that's what they have lower-level people for, and that's where you'll be sent if the senior-level person thinks you're selling. Your call must be focused around helping the executive with one of the criteria outlined at the beginning of this chapter. It's not about selling; it's about helping them *invest* strategically to achieve an outcome. Your voice, your tone, and the words you use must resonate with confidence.

When preparing for your call, the way you handle an assistant who answers must be the exact same way you would talk to the C-suite member, including asking the assistant the same questions you would ask the C-suite member. I would never expect the assistant to be able to answer the questions I want to ask the CEO, but that's not the purpose. The objective is for the assistant to realize I warrant the CEO's time, based on the value of the questions I ask and the insights I bring. You should never shy away from asking for a time to meet with the CEO or whomever you're trying to reach; the important element in asking is *how* you do it. If you ask for "just a couple of minutes, because I know they're busy," you will get a flat-out rejection. Asking in that manner makes it seem like you're not worthy of meeting them and that what you want to know could be better handled by way of email.

Conversely, you can't ask the assistant for an hour's worth of the CEO's time. Sorry, nobody gets that amount of time. Even asking for thirty minutes can seem excessive. The magic time is twenty minutes. Ask in a confident voice that you would like twenty minutes with the C-suite member. Twenty minutes is gold: it's not thirty minutes (which only their direct reports get), and it's not ten minutes, which makes it seem it's not important. And here's the beauty of asking for twenty minutes: calendars typically are blocked in fifteen- or thirty-minute segments. This means you'll probably wind up with a thirty-minute meeting anyway. You will score thirty minutes when, if you had asked initially for that much time, the assistant would have told you "no."

I know it may seem surprising, but I believe just because you have thirty minutes on the calendar you should not take the full thirty. You demonstrate trust by taking only twenty minutes. If the CEO appreciates the value you're bringing, they'll ask you to remain for another ten minutes.

The Magic Minutes

Without a doubt, the best time to get a hold of the senior-level person (or, for that matter, *any* hard-to-reach person) is between :58 after the hour and :02 into the next hour. This is the one time when a busy person is most likely to be between meetings. If the person also spends a lot of time on conference calls, then they are likely to answer the phone at the top of the hour in anticipation of a conference call scheduled to start at that time.

Does the strategy work? Yes! I've used it for years and have found great success connecting with C-level people in some rather large companies. On one particular occasion, the president of a large Canadian company with whom I was trying to make contact was not responding to any of my attempts to reach him, whether through the telephone or email. One day, I called him at the top of the hour and he picked up on the second ring. Needless to say, I was shocked to actually hear his voice. I am not a proponent of asking someone if this is a good time to talk; to me, this offers the person answering too easy of an out. However, when I'm calling senior-level people, I will ask. When I asked him this question, his response was a quick, "No," followed by, "I thought you were my 11 a.m. conference call." I immediately responded by asking when would be a good time to call back. Without a pause, the gentleman replied I could call him at 4:15 p.m. and we could talk. I called back then and we had a productive conversation.

Now, keep in mind I'm also very hesitant of asking when would be a good time to call back, as many lower-level people will simply throw out a time they know they won't be available as a way to get rid of you. Senior-level people don't operate that way. They have a high level of integrity, and if they offer up another time to talk, they do so genuinely.

There is professional respect you must display when using the top of the hour calling approach with senior-level people. Be extremely respectful of their time. The person answering at the top of hour may very well not be one to randomly take a phone call, so showing respect will earn you far more in the long run than trying to monopolize their time at that moment. Numerous salespeople with whom I've worked make it a habit to block their calendars once a day from forty-five minutes after the hour to fifteen minutes into the hour, just for the sole purpose of making calls to senior-level and other hard-to-reach prospects.

They Have Friends. I Have Friends. We Need to Meet.

With trust and confidence topping the list of criteria to reach the C-suite, it is often imperative to use networking as the way in. Fortunately, networking is easier today than ever thanks to social media sites, which I covered in chapters 17 and 18. Industry and civic events are certainly the perfect places to make connections with C-suite members. I can't begin to tell you the number of CEOs and other senior-level people I've met and with whom I've been able to network at various industry events.

Without turning this into a "fundamentals of networking" chapter, I'll detail the two things you need to be aware of when looking to connect with top-level people at an event: first, you need to be ready for anything, and second, you must be confident in the moment. Recently, I was attending a major national industry event. While walking through the lobby, I saw in the distance a CEO I was looking to meet. The time was ten in the evening and the setting was a busy hotel lobby, but I couldn't let that deter me. My challenge was coming up with a "value comment" I could share in an instant, if for no other reason than to establish a connection on which I could later build. Because this was a CEO I was trying to meet, I had done my homework and knew two things: the company had just announced strong growth in its most recent quarter and had announced a major move into a European country. All it took was for me to compliment the CEO on their move into the new European country and the strong earnings, and I garnered the much-appreciated "thank you." I took the moment to then introduce myself, and knowing the late hour, I left it at that. My brief comment and introduction is all it took when I saw him again the next day to have a very cordial three-minute conversation about his company and industry. From that conference encounter, I was able to later have an extensive phone call and email exchange, ultimately leading to a profitable engagement.

The key is to be ready! Opportunities don't follow a straight line. I've felt what it's like to not be ready. Early in my career while making a sales call on a major company, I ran into the CEO in the washroom. Needless to say, I was not prepared and was not able to take advantage of what turned out to be the only opportunity I was ever going to have to meet that particular CEO.

What is important with industry and networking events is to not attend them purely for the chance to meet a specific C-suite person. I've seen too many salespeople go broke (in money and time) due to attending too many events hoping to network with top people, only to have those efforts fall flat.

Even though there is a chapter in this book dedicated to referrals, it is worth sharing how to leverage referrals with senior-level people. Because C-suite executives are hesitant to allow new people into their worlds, many times referrals are the only way in. Referrals to the C-suite can take years to cultivate and many times arise more by accident than with a structured plan. Some of the best referrals I've experienced are relationships that first began when both people were at different positions in their respective careers. A good friend of mine who is extremely successful in sales has built a massive business around his college fraternity brothers. In the twenty-five years since he was in college, his college connections have gone on to senior-level positions with a number of different major corporations. Not only has my friend been able to do business with his frat brothers, but they also in turn have referred him to other senior-level people in other companies. Never discount relationships. They may not appear to be valuable today, but over time they can create significant opportunities. Remember, referrals go both ways. As much as you want others to refer you, always remember that you need to be as diligent at referring, as well.

One final approach worth mentioning is your ability to leverage senior-level people within your own company to help open doors with other senior-level people. There is something magical when one senior vice president calls another senior vice president. Call it the "secret handshake club" or merely a courtesy of the position, but it's amazing how one senior-level person can quickly establish a relationship with another senior-level person. You may need to prod and push, but I can't say strongly enough how effective this approach can be in opening up new opportunities.

It's a Long Haul—The 10 Percent Rule

In the end, you need to decide if it makes sense to prospect senior-level people and how much time you should devote to it. Devoting too much time to senior-level people easily can create significant short-term problems making your numbers. Developing relationships and doing business with senior execs takes time, generally three to four times longer than it does to develop a typical lead. Plan for this when building out your calendar. I frequently tell salespeople to never devote more than 10 percent of their time to developing high-level leads. Giving it more than 10 percent can cut into the time you need to develop business immediately. Assuming 10 percent of your time is all you can devote means you also can't have a broad-brush approach, going after everyone at every company possible. Keep your list tight to allow you to manage it effectively. Doing so will give you time to learn about the company and the people you're trying to reach. Thinking you're going to cold call your way into the C-suite and get the meeting on the first call is simply not going to happen.

CHAPTER 22

Getting Past the Shut Door

You have a lead you know would benefit from working with you, but they are not responding to you. We're being optimistic by even classifying these non-responsive people as leads. The first question you have to answer is, "Has the lead even seen or heard my messages, and what is their reaction?" You don't know if the person listened to your messages or read your emails, and ultimately what impact they may have had. Just because they didn't respond doesn't mean your messages aren't having an impact. Procurement agents are notorious for not responding, because many times an ignored message will cause a salesperson to panic and offer a better deal.

You are shortsighted if you think a lead is ignoring you just because they haven't responded to your one or two attempts at communication. Change up your methods by using the telephone, email, in-person contact, social media, and even regular mail. As you use different methods to reach the prospect, be sure to vary your messages—even if you don't feel they're getting through. The last thing you want is the lead to think you're a lousy salesperson, simply because all the messages you sent are the same.

One of the main reasons you should change your message is that many times a prospect chooses not to respond because they don't have a need for you at this time. Notice I wrote, ". . . at this time." Things change, and a month or a quarter from now the prospect could indeed have a reason to connect with you. Look at how you're communicating.

Are your messages about selling? People don't want to be sold. Your first job is to get the prospect to see you as somebody they can trust. Focus on providing the prospect with information they can use and will find helpful. One way to do this is by sharing insights that come from sources outside of your company. By sharing insights from other sources, they will see you in a different light than average salespeople.

There are some people who advocate sending a lead or even a prospect a message that is essentially an ultimatum of "respond now or I will never contact you again!" This approach is childish and stupid. What does it do, other than make the sender look foolish? If you look foolish, you'll definitely forgo any opportunity of having them as a customer in the future.

When Is It Time to Walk Away from a Lead?

Salespeople ask me this question all the time, and I'm always quick to point out that each situation is unique. The biggest problem many people have walking away is the size of the prize. The huge opportunity that would change your career is something you just don't want to miss. The same thing can be said of playing the lottery—the lure of the big prize is there, but so are the extremely long odds. Quit thinking you're going to be the one in twenty million who will get the really big prospect to respond to you. You may very well starve to death waiting for that to happen. When it simply becomes impossible to get any information out of the prospect or they ignore you totally, it's time to walk away as the only thing you're doing is wasting time that you could better spend on working more promising leads.

Spend your time working leads and ultimately prospects where you have better odds of success. I've seen far too many new salespeople get caught up in their own excitement and wind up failing miserably. Knowing when to walk away is tough, and that's why I advocate keeping your emotions in check and sticking with the facts—and the facts are what your plan says to do next. Yes, each situation is different, but if you don't stick with your plan, you'll always change your mind midstream and, in the end, you'll never know for sure what's working and what's not. Being an optimist is an admirable trait, but you can't let your optimism overshadow how you use your time. There is nothing wrong with walking away from a non-responsive lead. If they're persistently non-responsive, what makes you think they're even a lead? At the same time, don't let self-doubt convince you that you shouldn't keep trying to contact them if you know you can help them. Base your decision on the value you place on your time.

It's a Prospecting Pipeline, Not a Prospecting Parking Lot

Keeping people on your "active contact" list despite not having any success is only going to turn your pipeline into a parking lot. Leads and prospects who have not responded are not leads or prospects—they're suspects. You need to move suspects to your "marketing list," the list your marketing department controls. Most marketing departments have a regular process of sending "drip" communication in one form or another to this list. If you don't have a marketing team that can handle this for you, then you need to create your own list.

Building an automated email system for B2B marketing purposes is much easier than most people realize. If you're a small business owner, staying in contact with non-responsive prospects doesn't take much time if you automate the process. There are numerous email programs available at affordable prices to fit a wide range of business needs. For years I used Constant Contact and found it to be extremely efficient and easy to use. Due to the growth of my company and the size of the email list we maintain, we now use Infusionsoft, which I would recommend for anyone with more than twenty thousand contacts in their database.

The key is to email these non-responsive leads—not to try to sell them, but rather to keep them informed and aware of who you are and what you do. Provide them with content you feel would benefit them. You can write this content, aggregate from other sources, or a combination of both. Keep it simple, because you want to make sure reaching out this way doesn't require too much of your time. Keeping it simple also allows the person receiving the message to be able to read and absorb it quickly. Do not view nurturing this list as a key activity, because it's not. Your time is better spent dealing with prospects who are already responding to you.

Use your prospecting plan to guide you when you come back to the names on your "non-responsive" prospecting list and begin reaching out again with active prospecting efforts. The worst thing you can do is to move a name over to the "non-responsive" list and just leave it there. Doing this says you feel there is low probability to ever make this contact a customer. If it seemed possible at one time they could become a customer, it's probably worth trying a few different approaches before giving up entirely.

Pick a Different Road and Pick a Different Car

Just because you're not getting the response you're looking for from a lead doesn't mean there isn't another road you can go down or a different car you can use. This is when reaching out to another person in the same company is the right approach. Never allow yourself to think there isn't another way to reach the company you're targeting. As long as there are multiple people working for the same company, there always will be multiple people with whom you can connect. My philosophy is to first target the individual you feel would be your best prospect, and then build out from there if you encounter obstacles. The worst that can happen is you'll learn more information and have more contacts, and the best that can happen is you'll sell to a new customer faster.

Turning a Prospect into a Customer

You don't win any prizes when you have prospects you can't close. A few years ago, a friend of mine was downsized from his corporate job and felt compelled to scratch an itch to be self-employed. He chose to become a financial planner. He had a great personality and a great attitude, and the firm he was aligned with was excellent. Basically, he had everything going for him, and I predicted when he first started he would be successful.

A year into his new role, he asked to meet with me to discuss his prospecting and selling strategy. The first thing he showed me was an impressive log of people with whom he had met, which also detailed the number of times and length he had met with each person. I couldn't help but kid him about the number of meals he had bought, the coffees he had covered, and sporting events he had attended. This guy was living what I call the "prospector's nightmare." The calendar was full, but unfortunately it was full of people he couldn't close.

His problem was his willingness to meet with people again and again without a plan to move them forward. Making matters worse was his personality, which was simply too good! As a result, the people he met with weren't telling him "no," because they didn't want to let him down. The more I questioned him on his "prospects," the more he revealed how the majority of them were either relatives, friends, or people he knew from where he used to work. The people he thought were prospects weren't in the least bit prospects. I'd even be hard-pressed to even call them "leads." What he had were people who were willing to meet because they thought that would be the courteous thing to do.

My friend could not truly separate prospects from leads and, more importantly, he could not qualify the prospects in order to turn them into clients. There is nothing wrong with thinking people you already know might be prospects, but thinking they're prospects or customers without a plan to get them there is simply unrealistic.

He and I both felt he could turn things around with proper coaching. He even joked he would one day become a top producer for the firm. Unfortunately, the situation didn't end with him becoming a top producer. No, it ended permanently, because he couldn't make the shift from merely wanting to talk with people to turning them into clients. Today he is back in a corporate job, and my heart aches for him. Due to his inability to shift his approach, he wasn't able to achieve any level of success, and in the end he fell short of realizing his lifelong dream.

Tragically, this type of situation occurs too often. The salesperson has a great lead who might even somewhat qualify as a good prospect, but then the salesperson lacks the skillset to move over the finish line. Nothing can be more frustrating, and it's a key reason why I wrote this book. I want to give you the tools to get the leads and prospects that will keep your pipeline full.

And now, in this chapter, I will detail how to move leads and prospects closer to becoming customers. I'm all about creating customers! Leads and prospects are great, but they don't put food on the table.

But don't waste your time. Before you try the following strategies, you might want to refer back to earlier chapters where I discuss how to determine if prospects are truly prospects, or merely suspects.

SIX THINGS TO REMEMBER IF YOU WANT TO TURN A PROSPECT INTO A CUSTOMER

1. Never provide the prospect with enough information to make a decision without you.
2. Never allow a specific price to enter your discussion during the prospecting phase.
3. Never forget the most valuable asset you have is your time.

4. Never become mesmerized by the lead who claims they want to do business with you right now.
5. Never make contact with a prospect just for the sake of making contact. You must have a plan.
6. Never forgo the quick sale for the sake of landing the big sale.

If you adhere to these six principles, not just some of the time but all of the time, I guarantee you will be more successful. You won't get sidetracked as often, making you far more effective with your time. Let me add information around each one of these six points to help you in your quest to use time more effectively.

1. Never provide the prospect with enough information to make a decision without you.

When I share this one, salespeople push back, claiming that following this tip will only require more time, which is counter to everything I say about trying to *save* time. It does sound strange, but I would much rather spend a few more minutes with a prospect answering their questions to get me closer to a close than have them go someplace else after I've done a lot of work.

You do want to provide the prospect with great insights in your emails, voicemails, and other messages, but never leave them so much they don't need to talk with you. The driving reason to leave messages is to get them to see you as the expert they *need* to meet.

Often, when you are on a call going well, the prospect will ask if you can send over more information. Your tendency might be to say "yes," as you want to be seen as customer-focused. That's a big mistake. By agreeing to send them information, you run the risk of them making a decision without you. This is a much bigger problem than you might realize, and it happens to all of us for one simple reason: we want customers to see us as accommodating.

The solution to such a request from the customer is to say you *can* send over more information, but at the same time schedule a time to go over it with them. Send the prospect the information just prior to your call, which allows you to control the process. Do not allow the prospect to claim they're too busy to meet again or they don't want to waste your time. This is the point in the selling cycle where you *want* to invest time. Never forget: the reason you want to review the information with the customer is to better understand their specific needs and wants. You'll never know what these are unless you're in a position to ask them questions.

2. Never allow a specific price to enter your discussion during the prospecting phase.

The only time price comes into play is when you are narrowing the offering or closing the deal. I do want to stress the importance of finding out the person's economic drivers early in the prospecting qualifying stage, but you do not have to give specific price points to do that.

Prospecting is all about setting the stage by determining need and helping the prospect realize you're the only one who can help them reach their desired outcome. Start putting pricing options on the table during the late stages of the selling process, but never before that point.

It's too easy to assume that when the customer asks for a price, it means they're ready to buy. Twenty years ago that might have been true, but ninety-five percent of the time in today's climate, asking for the price early in the selling process means the customer is an economic buyer looking for the lowest price. When the customer asks you for a price too soon, you need to respond by asking them a question about the most critical need or desired benefit they've shared with you. Your objective is to get them thinking about *why* they're talking to you in the first place.

3. Never forget the most valuable asset you have is your time.

Remember my friend from the beginning of this chapter? I will argue that almost any salesperson, regardless of what they sell, can find "leads." The problem is these "leads," who you might think are "prospects," really aren't prospects at all. High-performing salespeople understand this principle better than everyone else, and that's why they're top performers. I can't stress enough the importance of verifying as early as possible in the process if the lead you have is truly a prospect. Your ultimate goal is to spend *more* time with *fewer* prospects. Think about that for a moment. What I'm saying is you don't want people who are never going to become customers to consume your time.

Every contact you make with a lead or prospect needs to have one goal: moving them one step closer to becoming a customer. If you can't move them forward, you must be willing to cut them loose. As I've previously discussed, cutting them loose doesn't mean you forget about them forever—it just means you don't spend any more time on them now.

4. Never become mesmerized by the lead who claims they want to do business with you right now.

The urgent inbound phone call is almost always a bad dream about to play out in real life. New salespeople, in particular, get sucked into this ploy. The person calls or responds via your website, claiming they're a motivated buyer. In that "selling second," you morph from being a sales hunter to being "ace customer service person." The moment you do that, you've lost in several ways. You've become excited over nothing; you've lost your sense of how to best qualify a lead, and ultimately, you've wasted your time.

The inbound "hot" lead might be hot, but it still needs to be qualified. Failing to qualify is failing to prospect, and failing to prospect is failing to close, and failing to close is failing to make any money. I can't make it simpler than that. I've watched way too many new salespeople become disillusioned early in their sales careers and quit because they allowed themselves to get sucked into the emotional roller coaster of the inbound lead.

5. Never make contact with a prospect just for the sake of making contact. You must have a plan.

If I were paid a dollar for every email I've received with the subject line "Checking In" or some other sad line, I would be able to retire. Voicemail messages are even worse. Anyone who makes a pathetic "just checking in" call should be sent to a barren wasteland as punishment. Will somebody please give me one good reason why anyone who calls themselves a professional salesperson would think a message like that would be effective? They're not effective with leads or prospects, and I'd even bet customers who view you as a friend find them pathetic, as well. If the call doesn't have a purpose, then why are you calling?

If you call yourself a sales professional, then you must always have a reason for your call. There is always a piece of industry information, a new idea, or an update to an earlier conversation that will give you a reason to make the call. Don't think for a moment you don't have a reason to reach out. Make the contact, and make the contact now! Far too many prospects fall away because the salesperson failed to follow up enough. Remember, just because you're thinking about them doesn't mean they're thinking about you—they're likely not!

If you are unsure what the call or email should be about, then merely use it to ask a question or two to gain feedback on what you've discussed in the past. The reason I like asking a question or two is I can use the prospect's response (or lack of a response) as a guide for my next step. The prospect who responds quickly is certainly a more engaged prospect worthy of more of your time. If the prospect fails to respond it doesn't necessarily mean they're not worthy of your time, but it can be an indication they need more time to develop into a customer.

A variation on asking a question is to email your prospect a document containing information they might find interesting, and then asking them to let you know their opinion. The fact you're now asking them to do something before responding can be another great way to measure their willingness to engage with you. Many times all it takes is providing the prospect with a few easy opportunities to engage in a conversation with you, and you can then move them to the close.

6. Never forgo the quick sale for the sake of landing the big sale.

I will be the first to admit this is one "never" I struggled with for years. It wasn't until I spent a lot of time with another sales expert who I respect, Andy Paul, that I came to fully appreciate the value of a quick sale. Do yourself a favor and read his book, *Amp Up Your Sales* (AMACOM 2014). It's packed with great sales ideas from a person who has been there and done it. A key sales philosophy Andy subscribes to is selling fast as a way of securing the prospect, with the idea of being able to sell more later. As tempting as it might be to try to land the truly big sale, there always will be a risk of not getting it—and then being shut out of getting anything.

The idea of getting even a small sale as a way of starting the relationship is excellent because it allows you to build on your status as a vendor or supplier to sell more. There can be times when this approach might not be appropriate, but that would only be where large capital expenditures are at stake and you must be seen as the major player in the market.

Your ability to turn the prospect into a customer is ultimately what will determine your ability to earn a living in sales. I can't stress enough the importance of ensuring your time and energy is focused on moving prospects across the customer threshold. The prospect who wants to continually wait to make a decision or won't make a decision for whatever reason must be seen as a threat to your time. The prospect must either move toward becoming a customer or move off your prospecting list. The worst thing you can do is let them remain at status quo.

Conclusion: Yes, You Can Do It!

You can read all you want about prospecting. You can build a great plan. But until you actually *do* something, you won't get any results. Prospecting is the foundation of the sales process. If you get prospecting wrong, you most likely will get the rest of the sales process wrong, too.

Each time I'm in front of a team of salespeople, whether in an intimate meeting or a large sales rally, my advice is the same: don't try and apply everything at once. You'll be far more successful taking one or two key concepts and putting them into play at the highest level possible. After you're doing the first couple of items well, then begin applying another two. The idea is simple—attempting to do everything at once will overwhelm you and lead to inconsistency. You may even feel the need to give up completely.

Sales is a great profession. With each additional year I spend in the profession, the more I come to appreciate it not as a job, but as a calling. I consider it a calling because it allows me to interact with so many people and, in turn, share knowledge with and gain knowledge from each person I meet. Prospecting is the point in the sales process where we get to interact with the most people, which maybe is why I enjoy it so much.

Let me conclude by sharing a list I first developed several years ago based on more than fifteen years of consulting with thousands of salespeople around the world. As you read the list, keep one thing in mind:

there is nothing on this list you can't achieve. The only thing holding you back is your own self doubt.

Ten Things Top-Performing Salespeople Do Regularly

Top salespeople . . .

1. Plan their weeks and work their plans.
2. Do not allow email and other routine activities to consume their time or their mental focus.
3. Have a prospecting plan they follow without fail.
4. Don't allow their time to be wasted by customers/prospects who are not capable of buying.
5. Continually learn and look for ways to improve themselves, and in so doing, look to others to gain insight.
6. Know the most important asset they have is their own time.
7. Treat people in their companies with the same level of respect, communication, and support they provide their best customers.
8. Push themselves to a level of standards far surpassing what others would expect of them.
9. Focus on goals in everything they do and understand how being goal oriented allows them to remain disciplined.
10. Have positive outlooks on themselves and their environments, never passing blame on others, but accepting full responsibility in everything.

Are you ready to move to the next level? It's your move!

Great Selling!

Acknowledgments

Two people to whom I can't begin to say thank you enough are Julie Sibert and Beth Mastre. I'm fortunate to have these two on my team. Without the two of them, I can't begin to imagine how lost I would be, and yes, they would agree! Julie is tireless in every way, having spent countless hours cleaning up my writing. Thank you, Julie, for putting up with me and humoring me through the process of writing a book. Beth, thank you for taking the lead when the idea of doing another book first came up. Your sense of what to write and who to write it for has been spot on.

Throughout life we're lucky to develop relationships with people who, over time, become such reliable sources of insight and support. In my own life, I've been blessed to have the support of a mastermind group made of amazingly smart people. My heartfelt thanks goes out to the members of this group, including Miles Austin, John Spence, Anthony Iannarino, Mike Weinberg, and Jeb Blount. Each of you is brilliant, and I'm pleased to call you valued business associates.

I couldn't do a list of acknowledgments without a special thank you to Jill Konrath. Our paths first crossed a number of years ago, as we had the privilege to share the stage together, and we've remained friends ever since that time. Jill, your prodding over the years and keen insight have helped me far more than you'll ever know.

Thank you also to my family at the National Speakers Association. For more than ten years, I've been part of this association, and the friendships I've developed truly do make it a family! What I've learned professionally and personally is far more than I will ever be able to give back to the association.

Now to the family members who know me better than anyone! Without a doubt, I married up! For the past thirty-five years I've been on a journey with my wife, Ann Marie. Her patience, understanding and, most of all, her willingness to put up with my travel schedule and obsession with work defies all logic. Thank you Ann Marie! And thank you to my two kids, Chris and Michelle. You two are tremendously special to me. I can't say thank you enough—as well to your spouses, who have probably realized by now that any of your bad traits came from me. And all your good traits came from your mother.

I'm fortunate to be surrounded by so many other talented people, who I'd list if space allowed. They have provided me with insight and support to make this book come to life. Thank you God for making it all happen!

About the Author

Mark Hunter, "The Sales Hunter," is globally sought after for his thought leadership on sales and sales leadership. His high-energy keynotes make him a desirable speaker for a variety of entities including Fortune 500 corporations and emerging companies and associations. His client list includes BP, Novartis, Mattel, Coca-Cola, and Salesforce, to name just a few.

Along with his powerful keynotes, Mark Hunter also delivers in-depth training workshops and consulting. He bases all of his work on his understanding of the current sales environment, more than thirty years of sales experience, and the front row seat he has had working with thousands of salespeople across five continents.

Mark Hunter is married with two grown children and the most supportive wife one could ever have. He makes his home in Omaha, Nebraska. (He contends, though, his "home" more often than not is seat 3D on American Airlines!).

Consider how Mark Hunter can help you or your organization by having him speak at your next company meeting or association event. His high energy and highly interactive programs can be structured as a keynote or training for a full day or half day. He can deliver these live, via video streaming, or through his online learning program, Breakthrough Sales Training University.

For your free thirty-day membership in Breakthrough Sales Training University, visit www.HighProfitProspecting.com and enter code x7c33m in the Breakthrough Sales Training University section.

To learn more and about Mark Hunter, visit www.TheSalesHunter.com. You also can reach him at the below connections:

Phone: 402-445-2110
Email: Mark@TheSalesHunter.com
LinkedIn: www.linkedin.com/in/markhunter/
Twitter: @TheSalesHunter
Facebook: www.facebook.com/TheSalesHunter/

Index